W9-AUY-399

DISTANCE
CASTING

This one is for Mom and Dad, because they taught me the important stuff.

DISTANCE
CASTING

WORDS AND WAYS OF THE SALTWATER FISHING LIFE

Sid Dobrin
Foreword by Flip Pallot

Sycamore Island Books · Boulder, Colorado

Distance Casting:
Words and Ways of the Saltwater Fishing Life
by Sid Dobrin

Copyright © 2000 by Sid Dobrin

ISBN 1-58160-100-X
Printed in the United States of America

Published by Sycamore Island Books, a division of
Paladin Enterprises, Inc., P.O. Box 1307,
Boulder, Colorado 80306, USA.
(303) 443-7250

Direct inquiries and/or orders to the above address.

Publisher's Cataloging-in-Publication
(Provided by Quality Books, Inc.)

Dobrin, Sidney I., 1967-
    Distance casting / by Sid Dobrin. -- 1st ed.
    p. cm.
    ISBN: 1-58160-100-X

    1. Saltwater Fishing. 2. Essays. I. Title.

PS3554.O27D57 2000   814.6
                       QBI00-500045

Visit our Web site at www.sycamoreisland.com

Contents

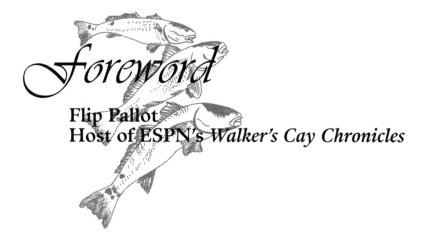

Foreword

Flip Pallot
Host of ESPN's *Walker's Cay Chronicles*

I hate it when someone writes my life! I really hate it when they do it so much better than I could have myself! Read *Distance Casting* and you'll share my feelings. Sid Dobrin is our brother, and we never even knew it!

The following pages tell Sid's story and all the while make us think about our own. Each of his dreams, each of his peeves, and many of his adventures parallel our own. His dad made me think of my own and fishing trips we shared and how much more than fishing trips they really were. His mom, like my own, encouraged the beginnings of his fishing lifetime and made me think of the many days that my mother dropped me off at the east edge of the Everglades at daylight and waited for me to canoe back to her flashing headlights after dark. His grandfather and his invention of the fiberglass boat (a story that I really believe) reminded me of my own grandfather and his invention of the electric gasoline pump (also sold to the military for peanuts), and Sid's understanding and description of friendship all combine to make *Distance Casting* a book to be read and reread!

Nothing is more entertaining that reading stories that share much more than the mere events that they portray. Nothing is more considerate than a writer leaving enough space between his words and thoughts so as to allow the reader to insert his own. Nothing is better than closing the back cover of a book and feeling that you were really there and a part of it.

In *Distance Casting* Sid quotes many of the writers who, with their words, painted the angling lifescapes that brought most of us to fishing, and in doing so, he joins their ranks.

The real payoff in this book is the ultimate understanding of distance casting, sight casting, and their respective roles in our non-fishing lives.

Thanks, my brother, for a wonderful journey through your life and my own. And Sid, I want to be there for that conversation with Buffett!

Without water, I thought, nobody could live at all.
—C.G. Jung

Good things love water. Bad things have always been dry.
—John Stienbeck

Writing has proven to be hard work, often painful. I can honestly say that I would rather be fishing.
–Linda Greenlaw

Acknowledgments

I would like to thank and acknowledge Anis Bawarshi, Julie Drew, Joe Hardin, Chris Keller, and Christian Weisser for their editorial comments on early drafts of this book. In addition, I am indebted to Carla Blount, who's assistance makes it possible for me to find time to write and revise.

I would also like to thank Flip Pallot and Karl Wickstrom for their support of this project and their suggestions about the book. I am particularly grateful to Jon Ford of Sycamore Island Books for his dedication to this project and for his ability to make the revision process as exciting and as challenging as the fishing and the writing (well, almost). Thank you all.

Words

"Why is it that every sonovabitch that can hold a rod in one hand and a pen in the other feels obligated to write a book about it?" my father asked me one hot June afternoon as we sat on the sun-bleached cottage deck looking out at the calm of Kitty Hawk's summer-green Atlantic. He was not angry, or put off by the passage I had pointed out to him moments before, just curious in his sometimes grumbly way. We had taken a few speckled trout earlier that morning and a few tailor blues soon after. But, the day had become such that by mid-morning sitting on the deck sipping iced tea was much more comfortable than standing in the sun surf casting. Besides, there would be plenty of fishing once the late-afternoon breezes cooled things off and the sun ducked behind the sea-oat-embroidered dunes a bit.

1

We had been sitting on the deck reading and sipping for a while, and I passed my father the book I was reading indicating a passage I wanted him to look at. I think the book was Howell Raines' *Fly Fishing Through the Midlife Crisis* or Jimmy Carter's *An Outdoor Journal*, but it may just as likely have been Zane Grey, John Geirach, Robert Traver, Nick Lyons, Crunch and Des, or the likes; I was reading a lot of fishing books that week—like all weeks. It was probably the fifth passage I'd pointed out to him in an hour; who knows how many that week. I wanted to share some of the magic I found in those pages with him, but he's not as easily taken by magic anymore.

I don't think he was fed up with me sharing passages with him; we'd always been pretty good about sharing. I think it was just a little tough for him to see the eloquence and philosophy of those who had found a particular happiness in the waters of the world and had shared it in pages of words. Only a few months prior, his mother had been diagnosed with Alzhiemers, and Dad had to put her in a nursing home. The recognition of what that meant had left him a bit more cynical than usual and certainly more depressed. It is a dreadful thing not only to watch your mother grow helpless, but to have to articulate the reality of that helplessness: that even you, her loving child, cannot help her anymore no matter how much you want to, no matter how much she helped you. It certainly made me fear the day that I may have to face the same recognition. Feeling helpless is one of the most frightening things we face.

But my father's grumbly question hadn't dissuaded me in any way from turning back to the pages in front of me and getting lost in the words. In fact, if anything, his question is an extremely important one and one that has plagued me for the past year. It is a question that others have asked often. It is one that writer and publisher Nick Lyons has asked time and time again in books like *My Secret Fishing Life* when he writes, "sometimes it appears as if everyone and his mother-in-law wants to write a fishing book." He also writes that "The mere catching of a fish is somehow such a potent triumph that it deludes all of us into thinking we know enough to write a book."

When I started writing about fishing, it was for fun. I had no career motivations about being an outdoor writer; I just knew that I liked writing and I loved fishing. The two seemed linked from the start. But my father's question sent me searching for a more elaborate link between fishing and writing. It sent me searching for some clue as to where the magic comes from—the very magic that sends so many of us back to the words of Walton year after year, or to the pages of our favorite outdoor magazines every month in order to escape the doldrums of phone bills and car pools. They are the words that leave us planning expeditions that will never happen, or even filling imaginary tackle boxes with outlandish orders from catalogues that our monthly budgets would never support. Perhaps the words of Lyons lend themselves to finding answers to this query when he writes in *Confessions of a Fly Fishing Addict* and again in *My Secret Fishing Life*:

> *In the best stories about fly fishing—by Norman McLean, Roderick Haig-Brown, Robert Traver, Sparse Grey Hackle, William Humphrey, Howard Walden, and ten thousand others who tell them in camps and at lunch tables but do not write—we find the best clues to why some of us fish. Odd, funny things happen; there is mystery and suspense, challenge and discovery; the words have the warm colors of earth and water, not the jargon of the specialist; we meet real people, with warts and wit and maverick gestures; big fish are caught or lost; people say wild and spontaneous words; events become memory and sometimes, in the hands of a master, bleed into art.*

Perhaps the words are the means by which we search for the whys.

My father's question still buzzes about my head like the tiny, winged bugs that make the most of North Carolina's hot June air, and the question has bit and bothered me like an iridescent green deer fly, not leaving me alone no matter how hard I try to rid myself of it. I had been working on the pages of this book and other articles and essays for some time, and this question makes me want to know why. Why is it that because we write and we fish we feel a need to write about fishing? And, why are we pulled toward sharing words about an experience that is for the most part a consuming individualized activity? Certainly, most of us fish to remove ourselves as far from the tangles of humanity as possible. It is an escape, an attempt to be as alone in the world as one can, to find out in some spiritual, primal way where we fit in the world, a chance to think about things, to get our heads straight. Of course, we may bring a friend along from time to time to "go fishing," but when we fish, we fish alone. We may wade ahead of our partner or quietly drift out of range of the other boats. The metaphors that come pouring out of the realm of angling are countless. We fish in order to help explain our lives; we fish in order to help escape our lives. Fishing is a selfish (last syllable emphasized, pun intended, and all that) act. I can live with that. Writing is a social, public activity. When we write, we write for others; our audiences are always present.

And words become magic. When the skies open up and the wind churns the seas, most of us take refuge someplace warm and dry. We're willing to be selfish on clear, warm days, or even a few of those days that leave us asking, "why am I out in this?" But few of us are selfish enough to risk real discomfort. So we run to the words that bring us as close to fishing as we can get without actually getting wet. We turn to Walton, Traver, Dunaway, Lyons, Carter, Geirach, Grey, Sosin, Morris, and all the others whose words bring us close to the experience in hopes of getting lost in the fantasy, in the escape. We subscribe to too many magazines; we read and reread our favorites. The words are magic; they take us to bigger fish, longer battles, unspoiled flats, and perfect reactions—the things that all casts, strikes, fights, landings, releases would be if we could make them so. I've spent my life chasing words, trying to learn their habits and habitats, but just as I think I've wrapped my hands around them, they slip through my fingers, they resist being caught. Words and fish—I'll always wonder which are the more elusive, the more dangerous, the more addicting, the more difficult to learn, the more difficult to catch.

But words are the chance to share, the chance to momentarily glimpse the magic of fishing that someone else saw. George Orwell writes in *Coming Up for Air*, "Is it any use talking about it, I wonder—the sort of fairy light that fishing and fishing tackle have in a kid's eyes? Some kids feel the same about guns and shooting, some feel it about motor-bikes or aeroplanes or horses. It's not a thing that you can explain or rationalize, it's merely magic." I wonder too, is it any use to try to talk about the magic, to write about the magic? Can we really capture it in words?

Orwell's words are perhaps one of the best descriptions of the way fishing enraptures so many of us in its magic, whether we are children of few or many years. I like his words. There are lots of writers whose words I like, and in the pages that follow I'll turn to other's words—words I would love to grab hold of and shout "there be magic here!" I'd be foolish not to. There are lots of wonderful words that have been linked together in fabulous descriptions of fishing, descriptions more magical than any I could ever construct. I can live with that too.

Angling is the most written about sport. It has been written about for longer than just about any activity. It has been written about in most languages; it crosses gender barriers, cultural barriers, racial barriers. It is perhaps as close to being a universal as is breathing. Perhaps that is why I write about it. Perhaps, because it is so much a part of the world, and at the same time such an escape from the world, we write and read about angling to give us a sense of where we fit, of where we belong, of who we are. William Humphry, in his book *My Moby Dick*, tries, like so many authors, to take hold of, to understand the link between writing and fishing: "I sought instruction in books—no other sport has spawned so many. The literature of angling falls into two genres: the instructional and the devotional. The former is written by fishermen who write, the latter by writers who fish."

I'm not sure where I fall in Humphry's taxonomy. I've been fishing since I was two, and my family has depended on fishing for recreation and, at times, for livelihood. But at the same time, my livelihood has been dependent upon words: I teach writing and I write about fishing. In fact, when I first considered writing about angling for magazines, I approached Jody Moore and Andy Dear—then editors of the Florida edition of *The Fisherman* magazine—and asked a simple question: "I've been a writer and a fisherman for most of my life; how does one get to do both?" They responded by hiring me. I suppose that in a lot of ways I slide between both of Humphry's categories: sometimes I'm one or the other, most times I'm both. What I do know is that there would be a great emptiness in my life should I lose either, and with both present, there is contentment and wholeness.

I also know that part of me is wrapped up in the oceans, but I have had to leave them for a while. Leave them, that is, because of words, the words I teach, the words by which I earn my living as a university writing teacher. Just before I moved away from my oceans, my grandfather asked me if I had been practicing my casting. Knowing he was setting me up for some punch line, I politely inquired as to why he asked. "Because," he said "even with your 15 footer, it's going to be a bear to cast beyond that second breaker from Kansas."

I was doing an unnatural thing in his eyes by leaving salt water. I was placing myself out of reach of important things, the very things of life. When we fish, we try to keep our physical selves as far away from the activity as possible. We keep ourselves tethered to the real action, the strike, by the finest line we dare use. We put as much distance between ourselves and our quarry as we can, only to try to make up for as much distance as possible as fast as we can. Fishing is the only hands-on activity in which we link distance by very fine strands. And by placing myself as far away from salt water as one physically can without actually working for NASA, I was moving to distances beyond the range of any monofilament or braided nylon. My grandfather's joke reminded me that part of being helpless is not being able to make contact, not being able to tug on one end and have the other end respond.

But being away from home waters and maternally comforting oceans has lent to interesting perspectives. I spend my time now wrapped up helping my students try to better understand and come to terms with words, and I spend quiet times alone trying to understand my own words. Norman McLean, in his celebrated masterpiece *A River Runs Through It*, writes: "I used to think the water was first, but if you listen carefully you will hear that the words are underneath the water." He continues, in beautifully constructed words, to tell his readers that he is "haunted by waters."

I am haunted by words—by his words, by other authors' words, by my father's words, by my own words. The only regular fishing I do these days is through the pages of other writers; the only magic I witness is filtered through their eyes, their words. And the pages that are filled here with my words have grown from the magic I miss and the magic that others are willing to share with me as I thirstily drink their words. So my answer to my father has to be that I write about fishing because it is not often that we encounter magic in this world anymore, but fishing and writing and writing about fishing remind us of what magic can be. They give some of us a chance to have a taste of control over that magic, an opportunity to wield words and share magic. And for those of us who would fish every day, but cannot because of weather, work, or other worries, the words are our casts, our sudden terror as line peels from a reel, our tired muscles, and our felicities of release. Words bring us closer to what we may not even be able to reach by distance castings.

Firsts

People measure their lives in firsts: first kisses, first cars, first loves, first steps. Most people take uncountable steps in their lives; some, like Neil Armstrong, Carl Lewis, Rosa Parks, or Fred Astaire are remembered for particular steps they took. But for most of us, it is our first steps that are regarded as the measure. We all remember the first time we saw the person we love most. Most of us are more apt to romanticize our first cars, though we've probably owned better, more reliable vehicles since then. Ask just about any American who the sixteenth, seventeenth, or eighteenth president of the United States was and they are likely to hem and haw and make a few guesses. But ask who the first president was and the answer rolls out proud and definite.

First man on the moon? First man to fly across the Atlantic? Winner of the first Super Bowl? First time you had a beer? First person with whom you had sex? First baseball glove? First home run you hit? First date (mutually exclusive of the previous question)? First apartment? First cigarette? For some, the first marriage? And so on.

Firsts are important. It is not that the experiences we have after our first are any less important, any less exciting, any less an experience. It's just that the first embodies an anxiety that disappears after the primary experience. It is as Hemingway writes in *True at First Light* that "there is a virginity that you, in theory only, bring once to a beautiful city or a great painting." In the second, third, fourth, and so on we have a better sense of what to expect; the sense of newness, of freshness, of the unexpected is slightly removed and diminishes each time. When we get up in the morning and walk to the bathroom, few of us look down at our legs and marvel at the wonder it takes for us to accomplish that feat—walking, not going to the bathroom. But you don't have to look too closely at a mother's eyes as she watches her child take its first steps, or listen too carefully to hear the pride in her voice as she beams to her friends for the first month "just look at him walk!" in order to sense the importance of this first time. Give that same mother a few years and point out that the kid is still walking, and chances are the excitement and awe of the first step is washed away. In fact, the chances are she'll take a few steps of her own away from you with a cautious look she reserves for the guy on the corner wearing little more than a single, well-placed sock. But dangle the child's first shoes— now bronzed to freeze that moment of first in time—in front of any parent, and it is likely that a bit of joy will stir as Dad or Mom remembers those milepost days. Jimmy Carter, whose words I admire and turn to often, once wrote, "One of the turning points in my life was when I got my first bait-casting outfit." I feel the same way about my first fishing rod.

My parents gave me my first serious rod and reel for my tenth birthday. It was a red Penn No. 9 on a stiff, four-guide pier rod, and it showed up about two months after my tenth birthday. Actually, on the day of my birthday, I found a sealed envelope on my bed with a card inside that my parents had made. It simply said, "we owe you one" above a picture of a fishing rod and reel cut from a newspaper ad. I found the actual outfit on my bed about two months later.

This rod was by no means the first rod and reel I'd fished with. Hell, Dad kept a closet full of old Zebcos and pieces of old Zebcos for me and my brothers, since it was safer to have cheap tackle around that would inevitably end up in the sand or overboard. And I know I had caught fish long before I was ten. Family mythology tells that I began my career as early as two when I would follow my dad up and down the beaches near Pensacola or Alligator Point dragging a plastic toy rod that had a small, plastic fish tied to the end of some twine. I've always found it interesting that toy companies make fortunes selling miniature plastic versions of the everyday items that adults would just assume not have to use: lawnmowers, dishwashers, shaving kits, cooking utensils; but I'm equally amazed that the plastic fishing rods—the one item many of us would love to get our adult hands on everyday—just aren't as popular. Family mythology also claims that my father, being the great dad that he is, would let me reel in croaker or dogfish that he would hook on his line, giving me the experience of catching real fish. He taught me how to hold the big surf outfit, his strong hands wrapped over mine, and how to feel the line for signs of a hungry fish at the other end. But being the insufferable fisherman that he sometimes can be too, he would inevitably send me off to search the beaches for the illusive peanut butter fish to go with all of the jellyfish that washed ashore, so he could pay more careful attention to the croaker.

But that first rod and reel will always hold so much more magic than any other gear or tackle I have ever owned. I distinctly remember coming home from school and finding it lying on my bed. It glowed with the shine of newness: black blank, silver guides held fast with red and gold binding, slick silver and red reel. Even the 15-pound, black nylon braid with which Dad filled the spool seemed too clean and new to ever tangle with the monster fish that I knew I would catch with this rod. As I sat on my bed battling imaginary giant black marlin in a storm-engulfed Australian sea, Dad and Mom came in to chat, and I thanked them with a sincerity that went well beyond the obligatory thank yous of birthdays gone by. They told me that they had also purchased fishing rods for my little brothers, and that I should not feel cheated out of a birthday gift because my brothers also got gifts. They explained that they had not wanted Adam and Ben to feel left out, so they bought them small rods too; Mom and Dad were always great about not playing favorites. When I saw the little Penn No. 77s clamped to the short composite Zebco 1070 rods, I knew that Mom and Dad meant what they said; these outfits were nowhere near the same class of tackle as what they had given me. There was no way that the same 15-pound braided line spun on to the free-spinning spools of these little reels could ever even catch the bait that I'd have to use on my gigantic, super-strong, red and black whale catcher.

But Mom and Dad had done good by all three of us, and those two outfits they bought my brothers still stand with the other tackle at my parents' home. I saw them there the last time I was in their home—a little older looking than on the day I first saw them (the rods, not my parents). One is missing the upper half of the composite rod, and both show the same signs of age that I have begun to notice creeping into many areas of my parents' home, an observation I am not sure I am willing to accept just yet. Home is still supposed to look like it always has; the safety and warmth of which should never be encroached upon by peeling paint and worn wood floors. The rods lean in the corner of the tackle closet, the same black-braided nylon, old and brittled on the reels, as though they are waiting for some other little boys to get bored catching croaker and toss them to the beach, momentarily forgotten.

I doubt if my brothers have the same memories of the day we got those rods and reels. Their birthdays would be filled with surfboards instead of tackle, their hearts enthralled by other magics of the sea. But, firsts are still important, and I recently overheard them talking about a new custom surfboard one had purchased and comparing it to their first boards saying, "yeah, but there's nothing like that first." That first rod was for me an important moment. It would be silly to try to explain the anxious fervor with which I begged my parents to take me fishing so I could get a chance to use the thing. The sorts of excitements a 10-year-old feels over certain things is beyond the defining words of an adult; it is the sort of excitement that will wake a child at three in the morning insisting to his parents that it is time to get up because today is *the* day. But like all children who are certain that if they do not take care of whatever is causing that excitement right then and there that they will surely explode and rain droplets of 10-year-old over the entire eastern seaboard, I had to wait.

When my brothers and I were kids, Dad used to spend two weeks of each spring in Guantanamo Bay, Cuba, teaching a class for the Navy. Inevitably, he would come back with stories of huge iguanas and great reefs for snorkeling, and I would wonder exactly how one gets into this racket called teaching. But the year of my first rod, his Caribbean course directly interfered with my chance to get that nylon braid wet. I spent hours in the front yard practicing casting that stiff rod with just a lead sinker. I could manipulate that level wind so well that I only backlashed the reel on every fifth cast or so. And, boy oh boy, could I send that lead sinker out there. All I needed was the opportunity to cast into water teaming with blitzing bluefish. But the chances of that happening before

Dad got back were slim. I do not mean to suggest that Mom would not have taken us fishing; Mom is as much a water person as anyone else in our family. With Dad away and her hands full with the three Dobrin boys, though, a good fishing trip probably seemed a bit much. But, Mom saw to it that I got that first time with that rod and reel, be it what it was, and where it was. There were no bluefish, no grander marlin, nor even a drop of salt water. Though the place was not where I had imagined my first fish on the new rod to be taken, there was a fish. Though I will proclaim repeatedly that place is so very important, fish are even more so.

The growing ecological awareness of the 1960s led the city of Virginia Beach, Virginia, to convert a 50-acre solid waste dump from an environmental disaster area into a recreational facility that became the pride of early environmental movements. The idea came from Ronald E. Dorer, who at the time was the Director of the State Department of Health. Dorer wanted to create a safer, more environmentally sound waste disposal landfill by building upward instead of digging deeper into the ground. So, Virginia Beach became the proud owner of a pile of garbage that measured 68 feet in height and more than 800 feet long. The mountain of garbage was then covered in six inches of soil. Just prior to 1972, the city of Virginia Beach purchased the land surrounding Dorer's garbage mountain, and by the end of 1972, the landfill area was turned over to the City Department of Parks and Recreation and dubbed "Mount Trashmore." The facility boasts fifteen sheltered picnic areas, five playgrounds, a skateboard bowl and slalom course, basketball courts, a soapbox derby track, four volleyball areas, and the only hill in the region—giving locals the opportunity to go sledding on the rare occasions of a beach snow. The facility also features two lakes: Lake Winsor, which is fed by the brackish waters of nearby Thalia Creek, and the freshwater Lake Trashmore, which is stocked by the State Fisheries.

The year I got my first rod, when Dad was down in Guantanamo teaching and snorkeling, Mom took me and my brothers to a picnic at Mt. Trashmore. I couldn't possibly remember what organization was having the picnic, but it probably unfolded like all of the Mt. Trashmore picnics of my youth: hot dogs, hamburgers, potato salad, soda, and chips under the sheltered picnic area; parents chatting as children ran over the Trashmore facility from playground to summit. But as the four of us left for that particular picnic that May afternoon, Mom told me to grab my tackle box and new rod so I could practice casting into the lakes at the park. Of course, when we unloaded all of the picnic gear that American families carry with them to ensure cluttering up as much of the setting as possible, the rod got piled against a picnic table with lawn chairs, coolers, frisbees, racket games, and tape decks. I had more pressing activities to attend to, what with an actual hill and other kids around.

As the sun began to slip away from the Atlantic and venture into the lower reaches of the western sky, Mom announced that it was time to reload the car and head home; after all, tomorrow was a school day. I protested our departure since there were still other kids there and since I hadn't even had the chance to cast yet. Arms loaded with picnic gear, Mom told me to run ahead to the pond that sat between the picnic grounds and the parking lot and cast a few times as she lugged the gear and my little brothers to the car. I sprinted ahead, knowing that when she got to the car I'd have to follow too, and begging for a few more minutes would be pointless, though I'd inevitably try.

After I'd reached the pond and looked back to see how much progress Mom had made in my direction, I quickly opened my blue metal tackle box and pulled out a Carolina bottom rig and a three-ounce bank sinker. I opened the plastic envelope of 100 K-Mart assorted-sized hooks that came with pre-tied leaders and selected two medium-sized hooks. I

15

snapped the wire bottom rig to the swivel that I had tied on the black nylon line that morning; I fastened the sinker and two hooks on the rig. Satisfied with the rigging, I dug to the bottom of my tackle box where I had stashed my secret weapon: a can of corn. Years before, my parents had taken us to Hungry Mother state park in Virginia for a week or so in the mountains. We, of course, spent a good deal of time on the lake fishing and encouraging Dad to keep rowing. One day as I sat on the bank of the lake catching crappie and sunfish on a hand line baited with night crawlers, I watched an old man cast out into the lake and pull in much bigger fish than I was pulling in. I watched for a while and noticed that the problem was that I was fishing with worms and he was using kernels of canned corn. I tucked that little bit of information away in the back of my head: in fresh water, canned corn equals big fish. So the morning of the picnic, when Mom hollered for me to grab my rod, I slipped into the pantry and grabbed a can of nibblets.

Using the can opener I swiped out of the silverware drawer—I threw it in my tackle box and to this day it still sits there unreturned, even though there was a good deal of fuss about its disappearance—I opened the corn and drained off the juice. I placed two kernels on each of the two hooks and cast the rig as far as my 10-year-old shoulders would allow. The sinker pulled the rig to the middle of Lake Trashmore, and I felt the line go slack as the rig settled to the bottom. I clicked the lever to engage the spool, turned the handle a few times to tighten the line, slipped a single finger over the line to feel for any tremors at the other end, and glanced back over my shoulder with hope that Mom was still engaged in prolonged good-byes back at the picnic shelter. Much to my disappointment, she was coming up behind me, and she reminded me that when she got to the car, I had better be reeling in and heading for the parking lot.

If there was anything that I understood about fishing back

then it was it took time and patience, and Mom's ultimatum didn't leave me with the opportunity for either. So I stood there watching her meander toward the parking lot playing chase games with Adam and Ben, knowing that it was my own fault for not having fished the entire day. As I sat there wallowing in a pool of self pity that only a 10-year-old could fill, the tip of the rod slammed into a bowed arch and the black nylon braid began emptying off of the spool with a roar of warning from the clicker. Instinctively I pulled back on the rod like Dad had taught me in order to set the hook, but the line was leaving a lot faster than it should have been. Screaming to get Mom's attention, I realized that I had set the drag entirely too loose, and I began thumbing it down tighter. I pumped and reeled so hard, knowing that if Dad had been there he'd have been proud of my technique—except for that continuous hollering for Mom.

Mom did come back over to me. She didn't realize I had actually managed to hook a fish in the 45 or 50 seconds since she had passed me, and was certain I had hooked myself or that some other disaster had befallen me, so she came running over. She reached me at about the same time the fish, who was putting on just enough of an aerial display to attract the attention of other people in the area, came flopping up the bank. Now you must realize that there is not a fish in Lake Trashmore that I couldn't have hauled out with that rod; after all, Dad had purchased it for the sorts of saltwater fishing our family does. So the 15-pound braided nylon and the stiff pier rod had no trouble whatsoever with the fish. It was far from an honorable fight on my behalf. But, I had a fish, and a big fish at that.

I'll confess: I know absolutely nothing about freshwater bass, and I knew even less at 10. In fact, at the time, I didn't even know what I had caught other than it was the first fish on my new rod. Since that day, I have taken no more than six bass from fresh water (and no other on that rod), so I wouldn't know what qualifies as big bass, but I know that was a heavy, fat fish.

I'm not sure what went through Mom's head as I carefully removed the hook from the fish's mouth and then stood beaming over it as it flopped in its death dance in the grass. But, I guess she recognized the importance of my catching that fish because she went back to the car, dug around in the trunk, found an old grocery bag, gathered up the suffocating animal, and put it in the trunk of my Dad's Pontiac. In hindsight, I can only assume that part of her motivation was probably selfish: Mom loves seafood, and a chance for fresh fish was not to be passed up. So, despite the day's gorging on hot dogs and hamburgers, we took the bass home to a second supper. I don't remember if I cleaned the fish or if Mom reluctantly took on the task, but I do remember that she battered the white meat, fried it, and served it properly with grits, greens, and sweet tea.

I know that when Dad got home tanned with tales of feeding iguanas bologna sandwiches, I told him of my conquest. I can't remember specifically his reaction to my story, but I'm sure he was glad he was not home to have to smell the frying fish (Dad, despite his admirable qualities of a fisherman, won't eat seafood, and hates the smell of it cooking). There's no doubt in my mind, however, that he listened patiently, smiled, told me "that's great!" and reminded me to be more careful about the drag next time.

I've fished with Dad and without him countless times since then, and countless times with and without that rod. But, even today as I take the rod from over my head in its rack and look at the reel in pieces in a plastic bag waiting for repair, I can't help but get sentimental about that first.

In some ways my nostalgic remembering of that bass is an opportunity for me to be aware of my own first steps. We all take many steps in our lives, and we take many steps as we evolve as fishermen. Thinking back on it now, as I sit in my own house, away from my parents' closet full of dusty tackle, I realize that the day on Lake Trashmore involved more than a first fish with a first rod. It was the first day I really ever fished without my father there as protective overseer. I rigged my line, I baited my hook, and I unhooked the fish. And what's more, I did it confidently as though doing so were the most natural thing in the world. But at the same time, I know that Dad was there too, in the knots I tied that he'd taught me, in my pump and reel technique, and in my eagerness to tell him of my adventure.

Perhaps it is that sense of adventure that makes firsts so important in our lives; the sense that the unexpected could happen at any moment—certainly a sensation that those of us who fish treasure every time we cast into the unknowns of the water. Will I hook a redfish, a shark, a ray? Will I laugh at the tiny rockfish struggling to free itself from my hook, or will I sweat and ache from a battle with a smoker king that should have easily beaten my light tackle? The sense of adventure keeps us coming back to fishing; it is one of those activities wherein even if we get familiar with the activity and the newness is rubbed away, we can still taste the traces of first by simply not knowing what the day might entail.

But there was one sense-of-knowing that I wanted—I wanted to know that I belonged to the world of sport fishermen. When I first got that rod and reel, I wanted more than anything to catch big fish with it; I wanted people to see me fishing with authentic, real fisherman's tackle. I wanted validation from the other surf casters who walked the beaches that I was one of them, not some little kid dragging a toy rod around behind him. And so in the months of the fishing season that followed my receiving that birthday gift, I took every opportunity afforded a 10-year-old to make that rod and reel live up to my piscatorial fantasies. It is those first chances I had to watch that black, braided nylon sink into the grey-blues of the Atlantic which stand out for me as crucial days in my evolution (descent?) as a fisherman. And like many of my early memories of fishing, of family, I'm not entirely sure what parts of my memories are memories and what parts have become constructed in my memories from the stories that my mother and father tell. Perhaps these sorts of stories are better left to be told by my parents, to be remembered in their eyes watching their oldest son take some first steps. Perhaps these are only memories I've created for myself from my parents' words in order to live up to the pride their voices exhibit when they tell stories. Perhaps the words and the family mythologies have themselves become the memories.

Each year for the last 20 years or so, my family has spent part of our summer vacations on the Outer Banks of North Carolina. We were lucky as children that our parents were educators, so their vacations were long and coincided with our breaks from school. This gave us time for wonderful summers together. Mom and Dad made it very clear to us that education doesn't just take place in the classroom, that the world is out there to be experienced. So, they made every effort they could afford to give us experience. I remember walking into the parking lot on the last day of school for many years only to find our motor home loaded and waiting for a six-week adventure in some other part of the country. We never even went home; from school classroom to world classroom in a matter of steps across the parking lot. We learned camping, outdoorsmanship, history, geography, and a slew of other things that we would have never picked up in private-school classrooms. There's no question that we were luckier than most, though I must admit the experience of a summer camp might have been fun too.

Even without summer camp, though, there was always the Outer Banks. When we lived in Norfolk, we were less than two hours from these barrier islands, so in lots of ways they became part of our home, our backyard. In addition to the annual trip, we would venture down on weekends from time to time, or if a big storm or hurricane had been through, we'd take the day to check out the erosion and damage, or if the news of blues crashing the beach reached us, I could talk Dad into a day of surf casting. Even as Adam and Ben and I grew into teenage years of more freedom, the Outer Banks would play a role in our lives, as we would take road trips there, or ditch school to go to the beach, or sit and drink whiskey in the dusk hues of college weekends. Inevitably, because of its proximity, the Outer Banks became a place where I learned a lot about fishing.

The summer of my tenth year, I brought my very own first rod and reel to the Outer Banks. No longer did I have to rely upon Dad rigging a Zebco for me, which meant I didn't have to use the bottom rigs and cut shrimp with which he insisted we fish. I could tie on a Hopkins No=Eql, and fish for the monster bluefish that I knew had to be in the water. So that's what I did. One morning, as the pink light of dawn pushed the greys of night off of the islands, I stood casting a two and a half ounce Hopkins' spoon into the rough Atlantic surf. By mid-morning other surf casters were chasing a school of menhaden up and down the beach, occasionally hooking small tailor blues that were chopping up the pod of baitfish. I joined in the hunt and pulled that huge treble hooked spoon through the darkened spot in the surf where the terrified bait were trying to dodge the razored teeth of the little blue fish. Because my lure was so big, and because I was pumping and reeling so fast in order to keep it from sinking to the sandy bottom, there was no way any one of those bluefish could have grabbed the big chunk of metal at the end of my line.

I, of course, didn't realize this, and became more and more frustrated as everyone else around me began hooking bluefish. All I pulled in was an occasional panicked menhaden that I snagged. I would toss the bleeding fish back to the surf disappointed that the tugging I had felt wasn't a blue. With each snagged menhaden and each blue that someone else caught, I grew more frustrated and more determined. Menhaden literally beached themselves at my feet trying to escape the jaws of the feeding blues. I marched up and down the beach following the dark patch in the surf. Other fishermen joined in and others left; the crowd around me seemed as static as the shape of the fleeing menhadens' pod.

I never left the beach that day. I didn't stop for lunch, and I didn't stop for supper. I just followed the slaps of bluefish in the surf up and down the beach. At times I would be miles north of our cottage and at others I'd be miles south. During my last visit to my parents' house, Mom reminded me of this incident. She told me that she brought me a sandwich at lunch, but I refused to stop casting long enough to eat. She said when I refused to come to dinner (a refusal with which I would have never gotten away had this not been vacation), she was angry and stood on the deck watching me through Dad's binoculars. She told me that the determination she saw in that 10-year-old frightened her; I imagine it would frighten just about anyone. No one should become that obsessed with anything, let alone a 10-year-old. I guess that for a mother watching her son take those first steps in such dramatic ways can be disconcerting, but then again, Mom has always encouraged us to take big steps.

I never did catch one of those little blues from the beach that year, though they appeared just about every day. Dad did take us to fish on the Oregon Inlet Bridge, and we got some good fish there (this was many years before the shifting sands of the inlet sealed off most of the waterway there and fish populations still moved through in huge schools). It wasn't until the next year when I acquired the first rod and reel I ever bought with my own money that I started catching blues in the surf. After nearly two weeks of watching other people catch fish right in front of me, I took mental note of the spinning tackle, of the bucktails and plastic jigs, and when I showed back up on that beach the following year I was armed. I caught over a hundred blues a day for two solid weeks that following year; each night I would mark on an index card how many of what kind of fish I caught. I wanted a record of my success, and that card remained tacked to my bulletin board in my childhood bedroom until I left for college. I have long since given up on keeping count, not only of fish, but of other experiences from which the confines of numbers distract. I guess I reached a point when being able to say "I caught a hundred bluefish today" seemed much less satisfying than saying "I went fishing today."

Those early days of fishing don't make for dramatic fishing stories; in fact, this is the first time I've written about that Outer Banks trip with the Penn No. 9. Other than a few stolen menhaden, this story is not even really about fishing, not in the sense that some editors insist to me that if I'm going to write fishing stories there need to be fish caught. Rather, it is about early impressions and first encounters with a wild part of the world. I'm often reminded of Aldo Leopold's words about these sorts of early impressions when he wrote:

> *When I call to mind my earliest impressions, I wonder whether the process ordinarily referred to as growing up is not actually a process of growing down; whether experience, so much touted among adults as the thing children lack, is not actually a progressive dilution of the essentials by the trivialities of living. This much at least is sure: my earliest impressions of wildlife and its pursuit retain a vivid sharpness of form, color, and atmosphere that half a century of professional wildlife experience have failed to obliterate or to improve upon.*

I think Leopold's got it right. Somehow those firsts can't be improved upon. Somehow those experiences remain crisp, and the links we have to those firsts make finding the memories that much easier, though memories they must remain. I can hold that black blanked rod, look at the wear in the butt, feel the scratches in the reel housing, and tug at the unraveling threads around the guides. But for some reason, even as I sit here in my land-locked home at 2:30 in the morning writing this, I have the urge to take the rod and put it back in its place above my head in its rack with the 20 or 30 other rods that hang with it—put it back with the other steps I've taken and measured. It is as though I want to put those bronzed baby shoes back on the shelf. The moment of firsts remembered and enjoyed; the measure of the first marked and noted. And having done so, I want to move on to the next steps, the next car, the next beer, the next fish.

Fathers

I recently served on a dissertation committee of a student who had written his doctoral thesis on the literature of fly-fishing. The project intrigued me since it's not often that the academic world in which I work overlaps the world of fishing in which I live, and when words become the direct link between the two worlds, I'm left with an excitement for both more than usual. I'm not sure whether there's a legitimate field of study here or that fishing belongs in academics, but I have to admit that the academy is certainly a better place when fishing is involved. And let's face it, Walton, Hemingway, Melville, Emerson, and Thoreau are as much canonized literature as it gets.

The dissertation itself was fairly interesting; it examined the history of fly-fishing literature in America, and the author, Mark Browning, has since published it as *Haunted by Waters: Fly Fishing in North American Literature* with the University of Ohio Press. Browning had also interspersed his chapters of literary critique with personal essays about his own evolution as a fisherman and a writer who deals with fishing. These narratives fit well as interludes and links between chapters. But what I found most intriguing was that the first and the last of these chapters discussed fathers in relation to fishing. His preliminary essay described his fishing relationship—or the lack of one—with his father, and the final segment explored his relationship and fishing experiences with his children.

Even now, as I return to the pages of my previous chapter, I notice an uncanny presence of fatherhood in my writing as well. In fact, fathers have become an archetype that permeates fishing lore and literature well beyond my accounts. Take, for instance the words of Jimmy Carter from his chapter "Fishing with My Daddy" from his masterpiece *An Outdoor Journal*:

> *Today, the most vivid and pleasant memories of my childhood are those times when Daddy and I were able to fish and hunt together, or ride along in a pickup truck talking about it. He seemed to love me more and treated me as something of an equal when we were in a dove field, walking behind a bird dog, or on a stream. In each pursuit of game or fish I had to go through a kind of apprenticeship, beginning when I was four or five years old, learning how to bait a hook and watch a cork or practicing with a flip or slingshot.*

There seems to be a variety of reasons why fathers are so predominant in the writing about fishing and our conversations about fishing. And let me be specific here for a moment: I'm talking about fathers and sons for the simple reason that I grew up with two brothers, no sisters, and know only of the father/child relationship in these ways. I have no children of my own, and to be completely honest about it, I know absolutely nothing about women, as my history of unsuccessful relationships with them has proven. This is, as we would label it in an academic setting, my standpoint. I do not mean to negate the father/daughter, mother/daughter, or mother/son relationships here, particularly since my relationship with my mother is equally as important to me (and she'd kill me for not saying so), and since there have been many intriguing discussions of fishing and fathers from other standpoints. For instance in both of Holly Morris' collections—*Uncommon Waters* and *A Different Angle*—images of fathers emerge, as do images of mothers as the passer of knowledge (particularly noteworthy is Lin Sutherland's "Abe Lincoln Fished Here"). And Browning's own final chapter addresses his relationship with his daughters.

First, and most simply, the answer as to why fathers appear as such a force in our evolution as fisherfolk is, for most of us, that we learned fishing from our fathers. They taught us the basics and took us on our first fishing trips. They were our mentors and our inductors into a special world. In a lot of ways this is a very primitive custom. In fact, in many ways I think that most of our links to fathers and fishing have some deeply ingrained ritualistic traditions that echo days when hunting was a necessary survival skill, and fathers who taught their children to survive ensured survival of the clan. Tribal leaders must pass on essential skills to young tribe members, both skill of survival and skills of ritual. My father taught me to fish, and his father taught him. As Robert Traver points out in "Sins My Father Taught Me," the opening chapter of *Trout Magic*:

In my father's favor I should add that he in turn probably learned his way of fishing from his own father, as I suppose most young fishermen do, and that this tends to happen for a variety of reasons: juvenile hero worship, ("My old man's a better fisherman than your old man"); plain and simian imitation; a lack of opportunity to learn any other way; and, more practically, the availability of his equipment when the old boy's off at work.

While this sort of survivalistic sharing of knowledge may be deeply rooted in our collective psyche, it is less of an issue today. Few of us need fishing skills for survival; though I would argue that the world might be a better place if we did. We stand to lose the sort of spiritual connection to the Earth that Aldo Leopold supported: "the danger of supposing that breakfast comes from the grocery" and that "heat comes from the furnace." Fish now comes in convenient pre-breaded, single-serving, frozen squares, and fathers need only teach their sons how to operate a microwave oven (and this we call "progress") or suggest what wine to select with the blackened redfish that the waiter conveniently produces from some hidden place. Luckily, my father taught me that you can't go wrong ordering Budweiser and/or whiskey; they go with everything. And women are always impressed when you order a bottle of Jack Black and two straws.

We have lost touch with where our food comes from. Children have learned to finger paint breaded rectangles to represent fish. We have lost touch with the sensation of meat. I happen to like the feel of meat, the solidness of its mass. I like the sensation of slicing meat with a sharp knife. It's very tactile—and deeply sensual. It seems very clean, when meat is fresh and knife is sharp, especially the meat of a fish. The slicing away of skin and bone. It is as much a condition of a good knife as it is of good meat, but knowing the meat makes it all the better. I think it is a pleasure we should all know, knowing what our food feels like, knowing the touch of skinning out, of fileting, of butchering. Tearing cellophane and styrofoam and cardboard just isn't as satisfying. Take Steve Chapple's words in his book *Confessions of an Eco-Redneck or How I Learned to Gut-Shoot Trout and Save the Wilderness at the Same Time* (a mouthful of a title) when he explains,

> *In fact, food does not walk onto the plate, in my experience. It has to be killed first.*
> *Even if you yourself don't kill what you eat, somebody else must. Your sister-in-law doesn't find shooting game birds to be a pleasant pastime? Well, has she ever watched cows being sledge-hammered at the slaughterhouse? This is what lies behind the waitress' smile.*

Nancy Lord in "Looking Salmon in the Face" has it right, too, when she writes about the salmon she catches and eats:

> *Our relationship to those salmon we eat—the ones we set fresh on our cleaning table and drain of blood—is something else. I slit their throats, and bright blood pulses out, drips like thickening jelly into the sand. When I rinse them with a hose, the bloodless fish react by twitching and tossing, nerved attempts to again reach saving water. I look at them, elegant silver salmon with scales like sequins, backs blue or gray, sides rounded or flat or limned with a hand shape, the almost grasp of a seals paw. Sea lice stick in restless hollows just fore of the tails, and the gillnet has scored the back of heads. The pectoral fins are stiff and flared, and still quivering. A silver-streaked tail is nicked. I look into the salmon faces, eyes, gaping toothed mouths. This one is snouty; that*

*one has a clear, wet, perfectly ringed pupil. This one
has fleshy cheeks, the other small, china-doll features.
Every fish face—every fish—is different, individual,
worthy of recognition.*

She goes on:

*Every year, when we remove the first king
salmon bellies from our smokehouse, we gorge ourselves on the fattiest parts and feel some small part of
tradition: the seasonal cycle of plenty, renewal. But
the next day we make lunch from grocery store food
delivered by the tender, avocados shipped thousands
of miles.*

She finishes by saying that "when we forget to notice the
rockweed thickening on the reef rocks or the inky cap mush-
rooms poking up overnight beside the trail, it's because we
aren't looking them in the face."

I like this. I think we lose touch by not knowing our
food, by not knowing that our food may bleed or spasm
before it dies. And I must confess, I like the blood, the taste
of it. My parents know not to throw out the blood, the drip-
pings from meat, because they know that after dinner, my
favorite thing to do is to take bread and sop up the blood
and suck on the salty, wet bread. It tastes like meat. This is
also why I prefer the taste of buffalo or elk to grocery store
steak (though I like a good steak) and why I like caribou
sausage. I want to know what my food tastes like. I'm glad
my father gave me the experience of learning to catch, kill,
clean and eat fish. There is something deeply spiritual about
the experience. James A. Swan, in his brilliant book *In
Defense of Hunting*, says it best when he writes, "To eat wild
meat is a sacrament for many people. It is eaten at special
times and shared with special people. Eating it brings back

fond memories and kindles a spirit of thanksgiving as you recognize the wild animals it came from. When I eat the flesh of wild animals, I feel different, more alive." We are losing this spirituality; we are forgetting to teach our children the importance of these connections.

But also rooted in the psyche of the American male are some difficulties in how fathers and sons relate to one another. While contemporary society may allow for more freedom of expression between fathers and sons—between males in general—than did society of 30 or 40 years ago, for the most part communication between men is a clouded, restricted area that fishing often breaks through. Generally speaking, fathers have had difficulty communicating with sons. Perhaps because their fathers shared similar difficulties, fathers and sons have been caught in a self-perpetuating cycle of non-communication. In a history of homophobic society where expression of emotion between males has been taboo, fishing has been an outlet of expression.

In many accounts fishermen relate of their childhood, fathers are figures who had little contact with the family, except when dictating from on high as patriarch. Again, Carter's words: "My father was the dominant person in our family and in my life. He was a relatively stern man when discipline and work were on his mind, and duty always came first." Notice Carter's choice of words: "father" when referring to the patriarchal disciplinarian and the more familiar "daddy" I quoted earlier when sweeter memories of fishing and hunting are discussed. His language is telling. Like many of us, he identifies a position of dutiful respect when discussing his father's strictness, but when the same man is referred to in context of fishing, he can comfortably say "daddy" almost in a child's endearing voice. It is comforting, almost pacifying, to imagine the former President's Georgia drawl uttering "daddy." There's an honest Southern nostalgia about the word that lets us show a childlike love for our fathers that we do not often openly articulate. With Carter, it is endearing to catch glimpses of the little boy that this great man once was.

Yet, these same traditional barriers that keep us from comfortably talking about our fathers with tender language also prevent fathers from making physical contact with sons unless it is to punish. The fishing trip becomes an escape not just from the confines of daily life, but from the confines that prevent father and son communication, father and son touch. Let me create a stereotypical father and son fishing trip to explain: one Friday evening, when father returns from work, he announces to mother that he needs a break and is going fishing up at the cabin with the "guys." Son, who has heard tales at picnics and Thanksgiving dinners about father's fishing trips, begs to go along, having been told in the past that he was just too young. Remember that for the most part, son only knows his father in the role of worker who comes home tired and leaves early; weekends are spent working around the house or on outings with buddies or alone. Mother insists that father take son, and father reluctantly agrees. Son is ecstatic. So, the following morning, amid Thermos bottles of coffee and nets and tackle boxes, son is awakened early and placed in the front seat of the family vehicle; very little is said.

When our archetypal father and son reach their fishing spot, be it lake, river, or ocean, they settle into their fishing, and father must first teach son how to fish. This is usually accomplished by baiting a hook, casting the line, and handing the rod to son who is instructed to hold the rod and wait for a fish. Father then goes about his own fishing, trying not to lose the solitude of fishing he seeks despite the presence of this miniature version of himself sitting and poking his rod tip in the bait well. Eventually, son tangles the line or tips the bait or ruins the lunch, and father is enraged and tells son to sit and fish and to be quiet and stay out of trouble. "Get somewhere and lite!" my father used to say. Son begins to regret going. Then, son hooks fish. Father rushes to his aid, hollers instructions, frantically tries to help son, and then nets the fish, beaming in pride. A high five or hug may follow along with a comment of "wait 'till we show mother!" And son is glowing at the acceptance his father has shown.

Okay, perhaps my "typical" trip is a bit exaggerated and reminiscent of Disney's version of Goofy on a fishing trip with his son, but it is not *that* farfetched. In many instances fishing trips become the starting point for communication between fathers and sons. When men are out fishing, the constraints that keep us from showing emotion in society are lessened—never totally removed, but lessened. Fathers may hug sons more readily with no one around to see that he's treating the boy with compassion; after all, we want our sons to be tough, not huggy. Even pals, whose only usual display of affection might be a high five during the game, will cheer each other on, embrace, and sit around campfires (god, I hate to say it) and bond, that is, share with one another. I know that I've had some great conversations with my dad when fishing is happening—not necessarily while we're fishing, but when it is the cornerstone to the day's events.

Now, I've been lucky; my father and I have always been close. There were certainly points when I was a teenager when we didn't talk, but we've been good about it for the most part and are getting better. I'm not so sure that's true about my dad and his father; sometimes, even today, the expressions of emotion seem almost obligatory, though I know they are heartfelt. But if you get the two of them talking about their fishing trips together, the barriers seem to fold a little. There are dozens of stories that have become standard material in the repertoire of my grandfather's fishing lore. My grandfather and grandmother built a house on Glengary road in Jacksonville, Florida, and it was there that my father, his brother, and his sister grew up. Glengary road dead-ends at the St. John's River, a mere block from my grandparents' home. My grandfather tells of my father coming home with a huge redfish one afternoon. He says that he scolded my father for fishing down at the river when he wasn't supposed to be fishing there. My dad insisted that he was punished unjustly for the incident since the fish had been trapped by an extremely low tide, and he simply walked out onto the dried river and plucked it from the water. To this day the two of them laugh about the incident, and the joy of the memory momentarily lets them remember and share with less constraints than they usually employ, and I'll probably be scolded for telling it wrong.

The seclusion of fishing often dismantles barriers between men; fishing is certainly responsible for my relationship with one of my dearest friends and my only real fishing partner, though I'll save that story for later. In the same vein, fishing between father and son often becomes the son's ladder to becoming like his father. There are few instances when young boys don't worship their fathers or try to emulate them. Being allowed to go on the fishing trip becomes a rite of passage, an opportunity for boys to say, "I am like my father." Even in my overdone stereotypical story, the chances are that son has begged many times to be taken on the fishing trip, only to be rebuked with excuses of being too young, of still being a boy. As I articulate in the previous chapter, firsts are important in our lives; they are the milestones by which we gauge our lives. Getting our first cars signifies a lot to the world (or so we think) about our freedom and our adulthood, and being allowed to fish with Dad says (mostly to ourselves) that we have become men like our fathers. As Carter tells it, "One of my favorite aspects of each trip was telling Mama and my sisters about my part for a few days in a man's world." James A. Swan also recounts:

I got my first real gun at seven. It was a single-shot BB gun, a Ryder, I think. I was allowed to use it only with my father, and we practiced in the basement for quite a while before he let me take it outside. I brought it with me when my father took me duck hunting, and I shot when he did. It was not really a lethal weapon for a duck, but I was very proud to be like grown-up hunters.

I remember very distinctly not being able to go fishing with my father one summer when I was about six. Dad and our next-door neighbor—and, believe it or not, one or two of *his* sons—were going to fish the Chesapeake Bay Bridge Tunnel pier. I begged and pleaded, but Dad was insistent that I was too young to be out there. The reality is that it's a great pier to fish, and Dad probably didn't want to have to keep up with a six-year-old instead of fishing. So, I got left behind. I remember being crushed. After all, I had been fishing with Dad countless times since I was about two, so why was I demoted to being "too young" this time?

That morning when Dad left early, I was heart broken, but not dissuaded. Before the day ended, I persuaded Mom (okay, *persuaded* is probably not the right word since I probably whined and begged all day until I wore her down) to take me fishing. With Adam and Ben in tow, she drove me to a near-by lake behind the Norfolk airport. This lake is attached to the Norfolk Botanical Gardens and has a small pier that stretches a few dozen feet into its muddy waters. Mom brought a Zebco that Dad had left rigged in the closet and introduced me to making bait from bread and spit—a skill she had learned growing up in Florida (on Mom's behalf, her mother used to tell me that my mom was so addicted to fishing that she'd sometimes be found fishing in puddles with thread and a bent safety pin using her patented bread-spit balls as bait). So, unlike the events of my first rod and the

Trashmore bass that would occur four years down the road, I was far from on my own on this trip as I dangled a bread-ball-baited hook over the edge of the pier. I couldn't tell you now how long Mom let me stay there as she and my brothers played nearby, but I did my time fishing that day.

That night when Dad came home with his cooler full of flounder and bluefish and he and the neighbors were unloading their gear in the shadowy lights cast from porch lamps, I dragged a bucket out that had one small, scared, freshwater catfish swimming around to show Dad that if he wouldn't let me fish with him, I'd do it my own way. It's funny now, in hindsight, to realize that's how so many of our battles have started: with me wanting to show him that he wasn't going to stop me from doing what I wanted. But that night no battle ensued. Dad took careful time to be proud of me. He, of course, asked Mom why she had let me bring the fish home and questioned what the hell we were going to do with that little thing, and she responded with a shrug of her shoulders that I had *insisted*. So, Dad and I shared fishing stories that night, and he let me help him carry in his gear. Later that night, after I had gone to sleep, Dad took my bucket-imprisoned fish and drove back to the lake to release it.

I don't think I ever actually had the experience of the first fishing trip with my dad in the ways that so many do. Long before I was born, fishing was already a part of my family's life, and by the time my first steps had my parents wondering where they'd lead me, I had already been fishing with Dad. But, I do know that the day he didn't take me because I was "too young" left me empty, as though I was not the man he thought I needed to be. Perhaps it was also that day that led to the sort of competitive notion of fishing I have with my father. There's never been anything said or openly recognized, but my fishing has become very oppositional to my father's. While he has always been content bottom fishing from piers or boats or beaches, I have been cursed with the want for big fish. Now, mostly, this is just part of the fever I have for fishing, but I also must confess that it stems from my need to unseat my father. Just as dominant males are overrun by younger pack members, I need to be a better (though that's really not the right word) fisherman than my father.

Dad and I have taken to pishawing each other when we fish these days. He'll sarcastically laugh at me for wasting my time dangling huge baits or dragging big lures hoping to get a single big fish in a day (okay, sometimes it takes a week or so), and I'll shake my head in disgust at his wasting time pulling in fish smaller than my bait. And yet, we fish. Even so, I find myself annoyed to see him rifling through my tackle boxes in search of a lure or a knife or some other bit of tackle. In some ways I feel intruded upon and very possessive of my tackle. I have spent years gathering my gear (I have an entire room dedicated to tackle in my Kansas home), and I am childishly guarded against tackle-invasions. Yet, I hold my tongue. After all, I used to hate it when he'd holler at me for digging through his tackle boxes. My instinct is to snap at that sort of intrusion, but my gut revels in the fact that after all of these years, he has to use *my* tackle to catch fish, that somehow I have superseded him as fisherman.

Now on the surface, that is ridiculously petty and spiteful, but like I said, it's an instinct I can't really explain. There is also a certain joy in having my father ask me to help him pick out a light spinning outfit because he enjoyed casting with mine. There is a sick pleasure I find in having more fishing stories (okay, more recent fishing stories) than he does. And what makes this all very odd is that fishing is the only realm in which I find myself having this sort of competition with Dad. Every member of my family is a teacher. My brothers, my father, and I have Ph.Ds; my mother holds terminal degrees in her field. There is a lot of respect between us, and none are afraid or stubborn enough not to recognize that in many instances it is wise to defer to another in the family for information. That is, we recognize that we each know more about particular things than the other. For instance, I would never make medical decisions without consulting Ben or Mom, nor would I make legal decisions without first discussing them with Adam or Dad, nor would they recklessly place a comma without checking with me. (The exception to this is my grandfather, who in his mind is an expert at everything and is undoubtedly the patriarch of Dobrin fishing.) But when it comes to fishing, a place where by default I had to begin my career in the shadow of my father, I now want to be head angler in charge. I have made it my domain, and his intrusion often leaves my hackles high. But at the same time, it makes me gloat secretly that I've attained that place; so, in respect and admiration, I hold my tongue and revel as he asks to borrow a particular jig or to take him to my fishing spots.

Of course, this is silly, and, as I've said, I really don't understand my own reaction. And yet, it's there. I love my father; I love fishing with my father. And, these words that I write here are the first moments of recognizing this feeling, publicly or personally. I feel guilty for thinking that my father could ever intrude in my life. After all, our lives have been so closely entwined that intrusions don't seem possible when you already belong. But perhaps part of why fathers play the role in fishing that they do is that fishing offers us an opportunity to confront our relationships with our fathers—often the very beings that introduced us to the contemplative activity in the first place, the very beings who told us to shut up, sit still, and fish. I know there are many fields on which my father and I disagree—relationships with women probably tops the list—and frequently we battle about those topics, but even more frequently those become the subjects about which we avoid speaking. I don't like that much, but when we do battle, we battle unfairly. On such issues, good argumentation is abandoned in lieu of emotional rage.

It's funny; when my father hears reference to someone

having a "relationship" with another person he always jokes that he's never had a relationship with anyone, since when he was growing up those sorts of self-expressive terms just weren't used. In some ways, he admits to not understanding about relationships, and echoed there I hear generations of fathers and sons who have not known how to relate to one another. As I've said, I've been extremely lucky. Dad and I are close; I love him and respect him beyond words. It's odd that I've made a career of words, but sometimes I find myself at a complete loss to find them. Thinking about Dad now, words become more elusive than I have ever known. I suppose that what I want to say to him now is that I hope he never stops digging around in my tackle boxes, and that we'll see each other catch fish many times for many years.

It's difficult not to wander into words about my own father and fishing; the two are bound in my life in many ways. It's hard to get away from my father; I have his hands. Quite often when I'm turning pages, checking the oil, mindlessly drumming my fingers on my knee, tying on a lure, fileting a flounder, slicing an onion, or shaking hands with someone, I mentally jump in surprise to see my father's hands attached to my wrists. They are strong hands that bring back memories. They are large and worn with big Southern-sun darkened knuckles and whorls and wrinkles deep and well defined. Mine are slightly more haggard, more scars and permanently swollen, with angled knuckles from breaks and dislocations, but they are hauntingly still his hands. They are the same hands that held my shoulders as I leaned to look down the Grand Canyon; they are the hands that held me in the water as I learned to swim; they are the hands that shook in anger when I upset him. But, sometimes when I am alone and scared, my father's hands creep out of the ends of my sleeves and remind me how to be strong and that I'm not really alone.

But, to be honest, it's not just my father's hands I've inherited. I look significantly more like my father than do my brothers. A few months ago, as a Kansas storm threatened the possibility of hail, I ran out in the splatter of rain to move the truck into the garage in order to avoid having to deal with an insurance adjuster, should the storm polka-dot the truck with dents. As I fumbled to get the key in the lock, I glanced up and jumped back when I saw my father staring out of the truck at me. In that moment before I realized it was only my reflection, I was so certain that my father was standing before me that the epiphanal moment that followed was mixed with laughing at myself and the terror we all face when we realize we have become our parents. Having had months to come to terms with such realization, I am glad that I have his hands and other features. I can only hope I have many of his other qualities and that I can resist exhibiting some as well.

I suppose in a lot of ways that's also a large part of why fathers and fishing are so intertwined. When we're young, we idolize our fathers. We want to be like them. We march around dressed in their shoes and hats, ridiculously too big, but we hope we can be more like Dad by dressing in his clothes. Then as years progress, we see the imperfections, the tensions, and we swear we'll never be like him. And then his hands grow out of our sleeves or we hear our mouths speak his words, his intonations, and we clasp our hands over our mouths and our brains scream, "Oh shit! I've turned into my father!" And after that settles in, we smile at it, and we are proud that we've grown up to be a man like him. So, fathers teach sons to fish because it is important to us that our fathers teach us. And men shift from thinking like sons to thinking like fathers.

My father recently had a conversation with a man who said his father was always angry with him. "So stop doing the things that piss him off," replied my dad. He said he realized his own thinking about being a father shifted one summer when among his three sons, one was running with the bulls in Spain, one was chasing hurricanes to surf, and one was alone in the Alaskan wilderness fishing (guess who). He said he was worried to death and didn't understand why his sons insisted on putting him through such grief. I guess we do because we want to be like him, have experiences that let us grow to be as strong as he.

I recently read somewhere that the number of anglers in the state of Florida has dropped by 10 or 15 percent over the past few years because access to fishable waters has been decreased to the point where it's just a hassle to find a spot to fish. Despite the obvious environmental anger I worked up over this, I began to think about the numbers of sons who were missing out on fishing with their fathers as well. I have had several conversations with men and women of varying ages in the past year about their fishing relationships with their fathers and with their children. Several have said that until they spoke with me they found it difficult to find pleasant memories of their fathers, but when they remembered those few fishing trips there seemed to be much more affection than any other time.

I have heard several people tell me that the only time their fathers ever hugged them was when they went fishing. I'm always saddened when I hear these stories, but what I find even more sad is that these same people admit that they have never taken their children fishing. I was talking with a friend the other day who is, as far as I can tell, a good father. He spends lots of time with his son and teaches him camping and diving and other important things, but he confessed that he has never once taken the boy fishing. "I remember being alone with my dad on a boat when we'd go fishing; it's really the only memory that makes me teary eyed when I think about him. But, I've never taken my boy fishing; we don't even own fishing rods" he told me. "I don't want him to miss out on that." I invited the two of them to go fishing one day, but the father never seems to find time to make the trip. I wish I had the same wisdom as Henry David Thoreau had when a friend of his asked as to whether boys should hunt and fish and he responded:

> *When some of my friends have asked me anxiously about their boys, whether they should let them hunt, I have answered, yes—remembering that it was one of the best parts of my education—make them hunters, though sportsmen only at first, if possible, mighty hunters last, so that they shall not find game large enough for them in this or any vegetable wilderness—hunters as well as fishers of men.*

My friend is not alone in holding those memories dear. Even Carter confesses that "many of the most highly publicized events of my presidency are not as memorable or significant in my life as fishing with my daddy." I hate to think that fathers taking sons fishing is an old-fashioned activity. I hate to think that we're losing that important moment when fathers and sons learn to know each other and sons get to be proud of their fathers and fathers of their sons.

Home Waters

John Gierach paints some incredibly beautiful images when he writes about water and fishing, particularly when he describes the St. Vrain, his self-proclaimed home water: "Of all the rivers I've fished," he writes, "the one I've seen the most of is the St. Vrain. It's a small one—some prefer to call it a creek, and it's hard to argue—that's one of the major feeders of the South Platte. My own hole behind a rock is the three-quarter-mile stretch of the main branch that flows in front of the house here, but upstream from that are more than 300 miles of forks and feeder streams draining several hundred square miles of northern Colorado Rockies. Rough figures, of course. It's a big chunk of land sloping over several artificial boundaries:

from Roosevelt National Forest to Indian Peaks Wilderness Area to Rocky Mountain National Forest."

He continues in several pages to paint the landscape of the St. Vrain in amazing detail: "At the highest elevation it's real postcard stuff: incredible craggy peaks with snow, boulder fields, and mossy-looking patches of alpine tundra sloping down to lovely, small, trout lakes, any one of which would look fine on a liquor store calendar."

I love how Gierach writes. He is, without a doubt, one of the best contemporary fishing writers around, and I'm certainly not alone in making that claim. In fact, I feel a little guilty borrowing and pluralizing the title of his chapter "Home Water" from *The View From Rat Lake* for my title. I'll rationalize and claim it as an attempt at tribute and flattery, but let's face it, when it comes to writing, I'm no Gierach. To be honest about it too, when it comes to fishing, I'm no Gierach either. He's a devout member of the Church of Trout and a purist of the order of fly rod. I am new to the fly rod, and the countless saltwater trout I've taken on spinning tackle aren't what Gierach would call trout. My guess is that Gierach would probably spit on my boots if he heard me refer to myself as a fisherman. I can practically hear him grumble something about me being too damn young to know anything about fishing, and the fact that I've actually used something as vulgar as 80-pound test would probably leave him questioning my ancestry. But that's what I like about Gierach; he's as fanatical as I'd like to be. I strive to that level of curmudgeonly purism. Many of my friends would probably roll their eyes and contend that I've taken the devotion far enough, but like I said, I'm no Gierach.

One of the things that Gierach does when he writes is he takes readers places. I don't mean that he simply describes where he's been or who he's fished with or what he's caught. He takes you by the hand and sits you down next to him and shows you the water until you smell it, taste it, and squint in the glittery reflection of sunlight. There are times when I read Gierach that my shoulders ache from the landing of a trout. There are times I sit smiling, exhausted, wanting to be able to pass him my flask in the glow of the campfire. It's amazing that he can make readers feel so at home with places we've never been. I like that feeling of home.

I went to my childhood home for a few days this past Thanksgiving, as I do each year. Clan Dobrin's Thanksgiving drips with tradition, most of which revolves around arrays of food and football and hours of eating oneself stupid. We make no pretenses about buttoning our pants. My parents' home always feels comfortable this time of the year. The Virginia air is shivery, but not unbearably cold. The backyard is covered in a crunchy carpet of leaves from the giant pear tree which closely matches the color of the house's hundred-year-old bricks. The radiators in my parents' turn-of-the-century house hiss and creak in a welcoming cantata. There's an overwhelming sense of safety within the walls of this house, like being a child again and sitting in Dad's lap. Memories dance about and seem to grab at me each time my eyes pass something on a shelf. Even the incredible smells that waft out of the kitchen shake free childhood memories.

Food, in our family, is a cornerstone of life. Food must possess two qualities for clan Dobrin to approve: flavor and quantity. We like our food to taste and to smell; we do not eat bland food. And, we want lots of it. I have not grown accustomed to Midwestern cuisine, the main staple of which is pasty cream-of-mushroom soup, and the local speciality is the casserole, an unidentifiable mush (which I have seen in various colors) baked in a ceramic dish. The bland casseroles, in fact, were what set me to understand why this part of the world is known as the "plain states"; the locals have also taken great offense at my renaming the covered-dish fodder "asseroles."

At casa del Dobrin, smells of garlic and onions, hot peppers, vinegars, livers, marinated meats, sharp cheeses, fresh vegetables, Greek olives, pickled fishes, spicy mustards, wines, horseradish, turkey glazed in garlic, smoked fishes, butter-thickened mashed potatoes, squash flavored with bacon, greens cooked with bacon, string beans cooked with bacon, bacon cooked with bacon, and jalapeno corn bread are always present. Mom and Dad taught Adam and Ben and me to cook, so all Dobrins are prolific chefs. But, Thanksgiving is Mom's domain, and she spends days preparing some of the finest food you could hope to put down your gullet. The only exception is that Dad leaves early Thanksgiving morning to bring back hot sausage biscuits from a restaurant so no one has to worry about breakfast, but since Mom usually starts serving appetizers around 10:30 in the morning, the biscuits are often still around Friday. From that moment when the first tray of succulent olives or buttery chopped liver hits the table, the eating doesn't stop all day. I'll confess, there's something comforting about sitting with my belly full and belt undone, listening to the contented sighs of my brothers and parents as we try to communicate through food-induced trances. It is the one moment when our usually loud, playfully, argumentative banter is rendered silent by slack jaws and lethargic eyes. Nothing quiets a house full of egotistical professors like a twenty-nine pound turkey. Home is good.

But this year, when I was home, I began to realize how much home was no longer *home*. At night, I'd lay in my childhood bedroom with my eyes closed trying to imagine what my room used to be like. It's been painted and there's new furniture. My mother's clothes hang in what was once my closet, and I'm sure she'll think when reading this that's she's robbed me of part of my childhood by making use of my vacated room. The truth is, I like it better this way. I like the comfort of the memory; it's much more real than the attempt to preserve the Sid Dobrin Childhood Bedroom Museum.

But this year, I began to notice the wear and tear that the years have inflicted upon home. The walls of the house need painting, the floor boards are worn past the polish at the top of the stairs, the plaster has cracked along the living room ceiling, and the windows have swollen shut for good. I took from the old tackle closet the old Zebco rods still stored there that Dad had bought to keep us boys from destroying his good tackle. Dusty, tangles of brittle line knotted on the reels reminded me of days of Florida croaker and North Carolina spot, and I thought a lot about home. And having been away from salt water for so long, I drove down to the marina where I spent bloody-knuckled summers scraping barnacles from boat bottoms and pumping fuel into boats of all sizes and shapes wishing I could climb aboard and go wherever they were going. On that brisk, grey day in November as Florida and Florida State battled on TV inside the marina store, I stood on the docks on the edge of the Chesapeake Bay thinking about all the time I had spent on that water and wondering if that water was part of what home is.

I know that the big blue waters that have dominated my life have been important in so many ways. I know they have been a resounding force in the lives of my family. But I also know that I don't have a St. Vrain; I don't have that single geography of water that is more home than all others. I felt at home on that dock. I could close my eyes and trace the waterways in my mind from that dock to my parents' house, to each island of the Chesapeake Bay Bridge Tunnel, to my friends' homes all over Virginia Beach and the Hampton Roads area. I could remember in which spots I'd caught fish and which spots proved barren. I could remember late nights on the water with old girlfriends and rough-water fishing trips with my brothers and father and mother. But I could also imagine the pattern of the tidal rush 90 miles away at Kitty Hawk, North Carolina. I could feel the early morning undertow tug at my waders as I dropped casts into the exact hole that I know holds dawns of speckled trout in early summer. I could hear the roll of the waves at Sebastian Inlet Fishing Pier in Florida as I flung three-ounce gold Gator spoons to the mouth of the inlet to drift over the rise where over-sized reds wait to grab baitfish on the outgoing tide. I could smell the grass of the flats that bespeckle the edges of Tampa Bay as it rushes into the great green Gulf of Mexico. And, I could taste the morning mist from a west coast Florida river that has become as much a home to me as have any of the other waters of my life. No, I don't have a St. Vrain, but I do have oceans of home and miles of shoreline that comfort me as much as Thanksgiving Day.

Two days after I moved to Tampa I was introduced to a nearby river that has become my favorite place to fish. A few locals once asked me never to write about this river for fear that the publicity would bring more people—the one thing that can destroy a river faster than anything else—or that if I did write about it, that I vow never to reveal its name or location in my writing. I will, as I have done elsewhere, keep the name of this river to myself. This particular river is different from other Florida rivers not in its natural composition or flow or fish, but in the fact that the commercial rape that has destroyed so much of Florida's waters has not yet found its way to this river. When I returned to Homosassa and Crystal River after 20 years, I was stunned at the numbers of houses, marinas, and other businesses that crowd the rivers' banks. And when I saw how congested with boat traffic these famous rivers were, I wondered how any fish or manatee or porpoise ever found room to swim. I suppose that the dozens of manatees that suffer the attack of boat propellers each year wonder the same thing. I'm not alone in my lament for what has become of wild rivers, nor am I the first. Aldo Leopold in his classic work *A Sand County Almanac* recounts:

When I was a small boy, my father used to describe all choice camps, fishing waters, and woods as "nearly as good as the Flambeau." When I finally launched my own canoe in this legendary stream, I found it up to expectations as a river, but as a wilderness it was on its last legs. New cottages, resorts, and highway bridges were chopping up the wild stretches into shorter and shorter segments. To run down the Flambeau was to be mentally whipsawed between alternating impressions: no sooner had you built up the mental illusion of being in the wilds than you sighted a boat landing, and soon you were coasting past some cottager's ponies.

And let's not forget that these words were first published in 1949, a year after Leopold's death. Unfortunately, we can say that things have certainly changed in the last 50 years, but not in the ways Leopold—or I—would have liked.

But my river had managed to avoid most of the crush of tourism and immigration. Traveling from its spring-fed head until it empties wide and clear into the Gulf is a trip into a Florida that my parents and their parents knew, of which I'll only be able to catch quick glimpses and memories in the words of authors like Totch Brown, Ernest Lyons, Marjory Stoneman Douglas, Marjorie Kinnan Rawlings, and A.W. Dimock. I can't tell you about my first day on that river simply because the memories of the many days have begun to blend into an amalgam memory. But, I do know that if I close my eyes, I can sit anywhere in the world and take an agglomerate of trips down that river:

At 5:30 in the morning, just as the sun begins to tint the summer sky in pinks and greys, the tires of my truck crunch into the gravel parking lot of a small boat landing and bait shop hidden under Floridian oak hammocks and leaning palms. Though the morning has only just begun, two locals sit at a wooden picnic table thick with years of brick red paint. The two, who quietly nod greetings in my direction, are several cans into a Budweiser breakfast. I pass this age-old tradition morning meeting of friends and walk past seven or eight barking dogs to a covered dock that lines the bank of the river. To my right, the water flows clear from a natural spring that pumps millions of gallons of 72 degree water into the river every day, no matter who fishes its water, no matter who builds what on its banks. To my left it flows for miles through twists of grass and dozens of islands until it spills into the Gulf. On this dock, I pay a dollar per dozen for live shrimp that are scooped from large aerated tanks and counted scrupulously into my yellow plastic bait bucket with the formalities of "they getting anything" and the reply of "yesterday they did alright."

With the bucket sloshing water and shrimp in the bed of the truck and the aerator humming soft bubbles to the shrimp, I slowly make my way down the last quarter mile of gravel road to the rental dock and camp store. Morning pleasantries are exchanged with the manager who drops hints to the regulars where the fish were hitting yesterday. I bolt down my Evinrude 15 to the back of a 14-foot fiberglass rental boat (still only $10 a day), and I slowly motor into the clear spring water.

This close to the spring's boil, the water is as near to transparent as is fine crystal. If the engine weren't running, the air would, at first, seem more silent than death and demand hushed whispers as though one were in an ancient library. But as ears become accustomed to this silence, sounds become distinct: the grass of the bottom gently brushing the hull of the boat, the squawk of the great heron, the soft hum of mosquitos, the splash of a solitary lazily leaping mullet that has broken ranks in the schools of hundreds that rush by in flashes of silver. And as the idle-speed engine moves the fiberglass hull around the bend from the boat dock, there is an eerie feeling of being alone in a primitive place. In the early morning air, thick fog hangs in the towering palms that line the shore. It wisps and drifts about on the flat clear water, its white moisture dancing across the burnished surface. I have seen the fog so thick that seeing the bow, or whoever sits there, is difficult. Looking straight down, I see the sandy bottom. Patches of grass bowing to the spring or the Gulf with the rush of the tide. If I look out across the surface, I see a flat mirrored image of the shoreline: colors identical, trees reaching down instead of up, birds flying below my hull. In the distance, the flat surface seems the color of finely polished wet slate, broken only by the occasional trice-leaping mullet.

I have seen porpoises this far up the river. Their blue, grey, and brown bodies distinct as they slide about in the clear water. They come this deep into the warm water to chase the mullet that school here. They come to other rivers too. At the Homosassa State Wildlife Preserve, the spring that feeds the Homosassa River is protected and is visited by other marine life. Snook, redfish, snapper, pinfish, sheepshead, black drum, and jacks come to the warm water by the thousands. I have seen schools of jack cravelle of 20 pounds that number in the thousands slowly circle the spring boil in a never-ending, circular parade. The first time I saw this spectacle of fish, I was emotionally torn between being grateful to no end that someone was saving this place from what had happened to the rest of Florida and the near-painful urge to run to the truck, grab a rod, and start casting into this pool of big fish. I was as frustrated as I have ever been; a starving child placed in the middle of a candy shop and told "no." The great Floridian naturalist Archie Carr recounts having had a similar experience: "I had heard that Homosassa was full of fish, but nothing anyone had told me was preparation for the sight I saw. . . . I stopped, and I stayed there looking for an hour or more, hardly able to believe what I saw and completely unable to understand it. The whole midsection of the basin seemed filled with fishes—hundreds and hundreds of them, big ones and little ones—of a dozen different kinds. And by far the majority were saltwater species." Carr was luckier than I; when he saw the basin it was not a protected habitat, and as he explains it, his "angler's instincts took over" and he ran to get tackle so he could fish this angler's dream. Lucky bastard.

Carr details, as only he could, why saltwater species of fish move into springs much like salmon move between saltwater and freshwater spawning grounds, though in the case of Florida spring water, no one is exactly sure why the fish do. Some have speculated that it is to remove a parasite that cannot survive in the desalinated water, and many have refuted this idea. But seeing the fish at Homosassa and having never seen these fish in my home river or in other spring-fed waters, I, like Carr, have to wonder if humans have either killed so many fish that they just aren't there to visit the springs or if we have overpopulated the springs until the fish are afraid to visit them.

My home river is lined with a thick Florida jungle. Tall palms and pines tower high above the water, and thick-trunked oaks form hammocks and drip with downpours of Spanish moss. Cabbage palms, scrub oak, and palmetto spears guard the forest floor, and ropes of vines bind the various trees and bushes together in an impenetrable net. All along the banks, trees of various sizes and shapes have fallen at the hands of the river's erosive forces, making the bank a thick knot of branches, trunks, and vegetation. It is a beautiful forest. I often look into this dense tangle and try to imagine how early explorers, paleo-indians, and others first saw this nearly impenetrable clot of plants. I imagine Spanish explorers in heavy metal armor trying to walk through the sharp palmetto in the heat of the Florida sun, cooking them in those uncomfortable ovens. If only that forest had been that much more dense, that much more inhospitable, then maybe Florida could have defended itself from the impending invasion. But like other colonized bodies, it could not ultimately defend itself. I am reminded of this each time I see a manicured lawn at an office building or public place where the spears of the palmettos have been clipped to remove their sharp points, rendered defenseless. And now there are few of these forests left. So, I look at this one and imagine what it had been like when this was but a small keep in a larger fortification. And I imagine how alone one would feel when first encountering this place.

Just as the sense of being alone becomes frighteningly belittling, a shack breaks into view out of the fog. It stands half on the bank, half over the water on stilts. It is old, perhaps from the 1940s or '50s. My mind recalls stories of fishermen and trappers who eeked out a living on these rivers. The worn, red tin roof is slack in places and the pitcher pump that is bolted to the porch no longer reaches into the clear water. Once, in a driving summer squall, I took refuge in this shack, hiding on the covered porch and eventually hauling the jon boat onto the porch with me for fear it would fill with rain water. The splintering wood stilts still stand firm in the clear water, though the floorboards have rotted in places. I want this shack to tell its story, to tell me who lived and worked there, to tell me who sipped on late-night whiskey and gnawed ho cakes on that porch and cursed small hauls of mullet. Two other similar shacks appear in the next mile of thickly vegetated shoreline, but this first red-roofed building sits in the fog haunting the memory of Florida's early years.

Small droplets of morning dew drip silently from the old shack's overhanging roof and get lost in the clear water of the river; only disappearing concentric circles on the surface hint at their point of entry. No windows line the walls of the old shack, and one wonders what transpired inside on quiet mornings of salt-pork and coffee before the day's struggle of hauling nets. These three shacks are crumbling reminders of the sawgrass-souled men and women who hammered out life along Florida's unforgiving southern shores. Now, farther down river from the old homes, six newer houses have been built, and dozens of black-winged anhingas dry their wings in morning breezes in an eerie post-dawn ritual. Wings spread wide to the sun, they stand in rows like black-gowned monks offering their lives up to heaven. I've never seen anyone in the newer homes, but the intrusion of building on this river will one day overtake it just as it has taken Homosassa, Crystal River, Alafia, Little Manatee, and dozens of other Florida rivers. One day, the remaining red-roofed shacks will be knocked down to make way for some concrete cube, and someone will wonder how they can get the anhingas to stop blocking the view.

Just as my small outboard pushes past these houses, the thick jungle of vegetation peels back from the shoreline, and islands of thick grass stretch before me. The clear water has spilled into a dark, tannic part of the river where gar roll in schools hundreds thick. The first time I came upon the rolling gar, I was convinced I had found the last holding point for tarpon by the thousands. I threw every lure and bait I had into the schools waiting to lock into silver kings by the dozens. The gar never bit, and it took me a full day before I realized what animal was making the slow scaly rolls around my boat. But these darker waters also hold manatees. The grass-lined bottom offers a buffet of vegetation to these beautiful animals, and I have sat for hours watching pods of ten or more slowly gorge themselves on a never-ending supply of river grass. Once, with my parents, we saw a pod of about ten of these docile animals. We watched them move about in the thick grass and murky waters for an hour or so, and we saw a manatee become agitated with another and thrash its mighty tail in an impressive display of white water. It is the only time I have ever seen that much activity from a manatee. They, like the alligators, have figured out that there's not much need for great quantities of activity if you've got a Florida river to laze about. It's a lesson I try to remember.

Spread before me now is the great green Gulf which meets the river in a speckling of seemingly countless islands, each of which is covered in thick saw grass. Few trees survive here where the salt water rolls around the roots of the grass. One or two islands, though, do have single gnarled trees, which make them easy to identify in this endless sprawl of backcountry salt marsh and gulf. I have given different islands my own names, not knowing their real names, or even if they have names. I call them House Island, Dog Island, Bird Island, Big Bar Island, and other nomenclatures that distinguish them in my mind. I have tried the names out on the locals, and some pretend that we are talking about the same islands. Others look at me like I've been mixing Jack Daniels with too much sun.

It is here in the twists of channels, oyster bars, and islands that I fish. Here the water is clean, the bottom topography ranges from pristine grass flats which hold trout and red fish to oyster bars which extend for miles and miles over the Gulf coast flats. When I fish here, I use the wind. I find a good drift and set the boat to be pushed along the shoreline. I have drifted this way, letting wind and water guide me through the oyster bars and past the islands, for as many as seven hours without having to start the motor or push myself free from a grounding. Drifting like this, I stand on the bow casting gold spoons or ZaraSpooks or plastic jigs or whatever I have convinced myself to be the day's magic lure. When I connect with a fish, I drop anchor and work that spot until I am convinced that it is time to move on.

Often when I fish out here on the flats, there are other anglers working the same skinny water, anglers more adept at such fishing. Porpoises chase schools of fish here. They will run right up onto the flats in less than a foot of water and splash ferociously as they push themselves through the grassy bottom. With tails slapping and aerial displays to put Sea World to shame, they hunt alongside me and we try to respect each others' space. I have taken to rapping against the hull in a specific pattern each time I see them, hoping it is the same group I see each time, hoping that they will eventually recognize me by my sound and know that I will not harm them. But we're not the only ones fishing here. Ospreys float above and attack the water with razored talons. Pelicans crash haphazardly about, and gulls screech around looking for crabs and shrimp or whatever else they can eat. I have even watched a beautiful bald eagle pull a trout from the flats and fly into a stand of palms to eat it. And there are massive sea turtles here, timid and curious.

But, as I've said, this is a place about which I don't write, or at least about which I don't write often or in the kinds of detail that would identify it. Unfortunately, others don't hold the same pact with this water. I recently came across a magazine article that named this very river and offered instruction on how, when, and where to fish it. This annoyed me. Annoyed me, that is, not in the sense that men and women who wear perfume to the gym annoy me (okay, men who wear perfume, period), but in the way that a single verse of song creeps into your head and won't shake free all day. (Lollipop, lollipop, oh lolly lollypop . . .). It's not that I was angered at the author for betraying the clan and revealing the secret temple; he wrote a fairly decent article that most fishing magazines would be glad to print: it had the how-tos, the where-tos, the when-tos and pho-tos to go with it. But it bothered me that what we do as outdoor and nature writers often compromises what we do as outdoor enthusiasts and naturalists. That is, the ethics of writing about the best place to catch fish or to hunt or to kayak or to hike often gives rise to those places becoming the worst places to fish or hunt or kayak or hike. As Nick Lyons tells it in *My Secret Fishing Life*, "Writers hurt a river by being its shill, its exploiter."

One place I fish frequently is the clam bar in St. Petersburg, Florida, and I've written about how to find it and how to fish it, as have many others. *The Tampa Tribune,* for example, ran a full page spread by Frank Seargent some years ago that introduced thousands to a quiet place that so many had overlooked before. Two weeks following the *Tribune* article, the clam bar was mobbed just as the Blackfoot River in Montana saw an increase in visiting anglers following the release of *A River Runs Through It,* as was the famous pond of *On Golden Pond.* I know that Missoula, Montana, has certainly benefitted financially from the numbers of anglers who visit in order to fish the Blackfoot and that you can't swing a Ford Explorer without hitting a fly shop. The numbers of people milling about Missoula's airport in their new L.L. Bean and Orvis digs holding rod cases is testament to the importance of the fishing industry to the local economy. But how important is it to the fish? Luckily, Missoulans are extremely conscious of protecting the environment and the resource it provides, but I wonder how differently the river fares because of McLean's words. Certainly the numbers of anglers who visit the Blackfoot would not be as great had McLean never written *A River Runs Through It.* Certainly not as many people would walk its banks or insist on the airport having more flights or the town having more hotels and more bars (and Missoula has some damn fine bars). In Missoula the beautiful words of McLean are responsible for the coming of people, as are the words of advertisers and outdoor writers who fill magazine pages with descriptions of how great the fishing is. And we have to decide, is this a good thing because economies flourish and people are happy, or is this a thing that places people's wants above nature's needs?

So this is what annoys me, this is what has returned to my head time and time again like the unwanted repetition of bad lyrics. There is a dilemma for those of us who are paid to expose readers to wild new places where the fishing is good: that exposing a thing necessitates that we make it vulnerable, particularly something fragile like the remaining strongholds of fish populations. The Keys, Costa Rica, the Chesapeake Bay, North Carolina's Outer Banks, Tampa Bay—I could list dozens of more places where the fishing's "just not what it used to be." And I have to wonder, have we as outdoor writers added to this? I remember what fishing was like on the Outer Banks as a kid; I remember campgrounds and long empty beaches. But word got around about the beaches, about the epic scenes of bluefish blitzes and red drum the size of station wagons, and now four-wheel drives from all over the country line the beaches in February and November waiting for the crashing beach assault by the oceans of blues promised to them by articles in magazines and newspapers. But it's just not what it used to be. And I suppose I feel as though I'm partly to blame. So it annoys me.

I have always wanted to write about fishing, and I love doing it. To me, there are few adventure stories written anymore that compare to a good fishing story: high seas, tired muscles, blood, pain, salt spray, big boats. I blame my addiction on years of reading *Boy's Life*. But I also know that I expose those places about which I write. In essence, I announce to the world that these places are ready for invasion. But, please, don't think me so pompous to think that I am some secret sentinel of these places bestowed with the right to defend them. But defend them I think we all must, as readers and writers. How often as reader am I also guilty of the invasion? How often do I jump in my truck and head off to some place I've read about where the fishing is supposed to be top-notch, only to find that my truck extends that line of rubber and steel that much further down the beach?

So it annoys me that I have no easy answers as to what I should do as a writer. Several years ago I went to hear Barry Lopez, one of the best nature writers around, give a reading. He read from his essay "The Stone Horse" about an ancient carving of a horse which he found while hiking in the deserts of Southern California. In his essay, Lopez gives the most wonderful descriptions of the carving, of its ancientness, and of the man who must have carved it. Like Gierach, he is able to walk you around the great carving and show it to you until you're certain you were there with him on that hike. Yet he is very forward in explaining that he will never reveal how to find the horse. Even when prodded after his reading, he resisted. I was truly intrigued by this loyalty to a place. He was sincere in his wish not to disturb that place, to intrude upon it again, nor to expose it to others. For surely, something as fragile and ancient as this carving would suffer from exposure. I respect this immensely, as much as I respect the ways in which Gierach can take us places without us ever knowing where those places are. I suppose in yet another way, this talent to keep anonymous a place and yet paint it so vividly that readers see it in the words on the page is the ability that I wish for as a writer. But as Heidegger argues, language both reveals and conceals. It exposes places about which we write, and it tells us things about the writer. At the same time, and what I understand Heidegger to be arguing, it covers what is not said; it serves as propaganda. It tells us a place is wonderful but conceals answers to other questions, like what has been displaced by building a new flyshop?

And so I am annoyed that I want to take my readers to places and show them, and I want them to call me and write me and say, "I read your article on this place, and I went there, and I did what you said, and I caught fish, and I loved it." But I know that even if one of my readers pulls his or her truck up onto that beach or wades on to those flats, that I have in some ways betrayed those waters. And so, I don't name my home waters, because just as we all want to invite people to our homes every once in a while to show them off, we don't want our guests to stay. And we sure don't want them to move in.

Partners

Soon after I moved to Tampa in 1991, I met two guys who would become two of my closest, dearest friends: Rob and Jason (known hereafter as Jota). As important as these two are in my life, their role here is minimal; in fact, their role here is merely that they were responsible for telling me that their good friend Roy was pissed at them for spending time with me rather than with him. Roy, it turns out, likes having few close friends, but wants them to be close at all times. I had robbed him of Rob and Jota and was rapidly becoming his least favorite person for doing so. When I heard this, I responded that Roy seemed pretty childish; I had not even met him before. But one sunny south Florida weekend, Rob, Jota, and I planned to go fishing in south St.

Petersburg at a spot Rob and Roy had discovered. Word spread about our plans, and by the time the weekend rolled around, I was outfitting seven or eight other guys who wanted to go too. Of course, Roy wasn't going to miss the outing, and he piled into one of the three cars in the caravan without ever speaking a word to me.

When our crowd hit the little beach at Pass-a-Grille, Florida, it became evident that Roy and I were the only ones who had brought tackle to outfit the expedition, and we were the only ones who had the slightest idea of how to fish. We instantly took on the role of guides and spent the day running up and down the beach attending to lure selections, tangles, baits, hooked sailcats, tangled pelicans, and the other problems that arise when you're watching first-time anglers fish with your own precious tackle: "DON'T PUT THAT IN THE SAND!!" As we moved from problem to problem, Roy and I ignored one another. It was obvious that I had walked into his world unwelcome. But when we found ourselves coaching Rob on how to handle a fairly large jack that had slammed a red and white Rat-L-Trap he had been working along the channel ledge, it became obvious that the barriers were going to have to come down.

In a lot of ways the relationships that grow from fishing—like those we build with our fathers—grow in ways that are not typical of other friendships. And, from time to time, they grow beyond friendships into partnerships. I find it particularly telling that in this day of politically correct language, we have taken to calling one's significant other that person's "partner." I think that the word itself carries too much baggage of business partnerships, formal, contractual bonds, but we've tried to make "partners" a much more intimate relationship.

That's what happened with me and Roy; we became partners—fishing partners, friends. We have reached an intimacy that only two close friends could reach if they spent countless hours on the water together waiting for something to happen.

When partnership is achieved, fishing becomes a crisper experience. I think of the words of John Gierach as he describes time and time again his relationship with A.K. The awareness of where and how the other will be fishing, the acceptance of the presence of an outsider in an activity that is solely an individual endeavor, the comradery of the conversations that follow a trip or make up the planning of an adventure—I think the sharing of adventure with a fishing partner makes having a fishing partner worth everything. You learn how the other thinks, reacts, casts, steers the boat, packs the tackle, makes the sandwiches. In those moments when you don't have to call for the net, because you know your partner has instinctively brought in all other lines and is waiting with gaff or net, then you appreciate partnership. When you stand to lose a big cobia or shark or king because the guy with whom you're fishing hasn't brought in the other lines that are now tangled around your leader and you have to holler again and again for him to get a net or gaff, then you wish you had a second version of yourself to be ready to do what you know needs to be done. Roy and I fish in that kind of synchrony, but it took a lot to get there.

When Roy and I first started fishing together, we were both fairly new to the west coast of Florida. My family was from north-east Florida (we were transplanted to Virginia when Dad and Mom took jobs there—I was five), and Roy's family was from west-central Florida, though, because of his father's military career, he was raised in Alaska and Kansas (he understands my suffering). So just as we were exploring the boundaries of a new friendship, we explored the local waters for places to fish. From the beginning, Roy and I fished similarly; we spoke the same language, respected the same tackle, and lusted after fishing to perhaps unhealthy levels. When I first met Roy's wife Stormy, Roy and I had been fishing everyday for a week. Needless to say, Stormy was not pleased that I had taken her husband from her, and it took us a while to hammer out how we were going to share Roy. Stormy, by the way, is a wonderful wife and mother, a dear friend, and also the only person who knows how to handle Roy's stubbornness. Their partnership exceeds any that I could ever hope to achieve with any other human being. They are, in the truest sense of it, soul mates.

Undoubtedly, Roy and I were meant to fish together; to be honest, though, the problem is that at the start we fished badly together. Early in our fishing, Roy and I shared a "just-in-case" mentality about fishing. That is, no matter where we were fishing or what we were fishing for, be it from pier, bridge, boat, or beach for Spanish, blues, reds, kings, jacks, trout, snook, cobia, or even bait (as I'll explain in a moment), Roy and I wanted to be prepared for absolutely any fishing situation that we might encounter. Doug Larson once wrote, "If people concentrated on the really important things in life, there'd be a shortage of fishing poles." Roy and I took that philosophy to the extreme. A typical trip might find us carrying between 25 and 30 rods, six or seven tackle boxes, coolers, buckets, aerators, tarps, gaffs, nets, and so on. The way we figured it was that if we showed up with light spinning tackle for Spanish mackerel, that would be the day the big tarpon or cobia were stacked up under the bridge, and we weren't about to miss out on an opportunity because we were unprepared— Boy Scouts beyond the extreme.

I distinctly remember one blazing July day when I was to meet Roy at the far end of the Skyway fishing pier (about a mile and a half walk from the parking lot) in St. Petersburg for an afternoon of clothespin rigs and, with luck, a few kingfish. The Skyway pier is actually a section of the old bridge that was left up when the new bridge was constructed across the mouth of Tampa Bay. It stretches right out into the main channel where Tampa Bay empties into the Gulf of Mexico and is one of the few places where anglers who don't have access to deep water by boat can fish for larger species of fish like tarpon and cobia and kingfish. It has been converted into a beautiful fishing facility, but when Roy and I fished it, it was just a crumbling old bridge. Now you can drive out to your spot, but back then a fence prevented vehicle access and walking with gear in tow through broken glass and rotting sailcats and skates was the only way to get out to deep water.

On this particularly hot July day, I did not want to miss out on any chance for any sort of fishing, so I literally tied tackle boxes, rod cases, and coolers to my back as though I were a pack mule. I was carrying at least a dozen rods, three aerated bait buckets, rope, gaffs, a cooler for food and drink, an empty cooler for keeping fish, several tackle boxes, and a tarp to cover everything should the common South Florida afternoon thunderstorms move across the bridge. By the time I reached the end of the pier, I was roasted to well-done by the hundred degree plus summer sun, I was dehydrated, the typical storm clouds were starting to appear far off in the western sky, and Roy was nowhere to be seen. I waited for an hour, but Roy never showed. I was so uncomfortably hot and tired that I thought I'd drop from heat exhaustion. I lugged everything back to the car, poured three cold Mountain Dews down my gullet, and drove home to kill Roy.

Our packing was a great source of humor for Stormy— and just about anyone who saw us making our way onto a pier or bridge or boat. We carried so much gear, in fact, that we spent countless hours designing carts and floating trailers that would make hauling our gear easier. In the end, we found that a couple of shopping carts were the best bet.

I suppose that part of our reason for carrying so much tackle was that for the first times in our lives we could *have* so much tackle. We weren't bound by parental restrictions on purchasing, and we were both students with jobs that allowed us to buy tackle if we were willing to give up some other luxury like rent or food. And to make the temptation worse, there are some great tackle shops in Florida. Kids in candy stores.

But Stormy was not keen on our addictions, and Roy was a bad liar when it came to keeping his purchases secret from her. That is, Roy is perhaps the most inept liar in America today, which has not only caused some problems with Stormy, but also affected his reputation as a fisherman. Just before Roy's birthday one year, Stormy asked me to help her pick out some tackle to give him. She pulled some lures from the shelves of a local tackle shop Roy and I particularly liked and asked what I thought. I told her not to bother since Roy had just ordered those from Cabella's a week before. Stormy never batted an eye. Three weeks later, when the Cabella's order arrived, she was the only one home to receive the delivery, which she signed for and hid. Later that evening, with Rob and Jota present to witness the event, she asked Roy if he had ordered any tackle recently. Fearing for his life for breaking their agreement about budget and tackle, Roy lied and said no. Stormy then produced the Cabella's box and asked for an explanation.

Roy was caught red-handed with the evidence displayed before him. Any sane male would have dropped to his knees and begged his wife for forgiveness, but not Roy. He went into full-fledged bad lying mode. Roy, with a poker face that I'd love to see across the table from me in a high stakes game, scrambled for words, hemmed and hawed, and told Stormy that Cabella's must have made a mistake and forwarded an order of his dad's (who has the same name) to the wrong address. Great answer, Roy. Of course, Stormy had known all along, since I never knew I was supposed to keep his purchases quiet, and I had mentioned it weeks before in the tackle shop. So, Roy just kept on digging. To this day, Stormy simply reminds him of the incident any time he starts to stutter in explaining something to her. Lying to any wife seems dangerous to me; lying to Stormy could be deadly.

Roy and I would share plenty of equally funny moments while fishing: we watched a drunk try to evade the police on

Pier 60 in Clearwater one night by pretending to fish. Eventually the cops left and the drunk staggered back by us, nearly spilling our three tackle boxes over the edge (we learned to downsize after a while), and we thought about pitching him into the Gulf of Mexico. But often even our most hysterical moments seemed less than funny when they happened.

One summer, when I was writing for *The Fisherman* magazine, Roy and I took a long-range party boat trip out to the middle grounds. Since the trip was costing us a bit, and since I wanted to get a story out of it, we decided to put in some time researching the fishing methods used on board so we would have every opportunity to catch big fish. We talked to passengers on the boat for weeks, asking as to best type of tackle, best baits, best lures, best approaches. We learned that for the big amberjack, cobia, snapper, and grouper, live bait worked best. But when we found out that live pinfish would cost us seven dollars a dozen and we'd need at least four dozen each, we decided it wasn't worth the extra cash from our student loans. So, as any despicable angler would do, one afternoon we followed the guy who sold the pinfish to where he caught his, and we decided to catch our own.

On the day we were to leave on the three-day trip, Roy and I made our way to the Ten Cent bridge just outside of Fort DeSoto in St. Petersburg. We rigged spinning gear with rows of hooks and baited them with chunks of shrimp. We were set to fill the huge aerated bait wells we had purchased (for more than the bait would have cost us at the dock) with enough bait to feed every AJ in the gulf. Unfortunately, the grunts and pinfish weren't too keen on our agenda. With only a couple of hours before the party boat was scheduled to leave, and with only three or four pinfish in the buckets, Roy and I were trying to figure how we could afford to purchase bait. The Florida summer sun had us cooked and cranky as well.

As we talked, I had a slight tug, followed by the dead weight fight of a good sized sailcat. We had managed to catch dozens of the annoying fish, so this one just added insult to the day's fishing for bait. When I unhooked the slimy bugger, it dropped to the concrete bridge walkway and didn't flop into the water. Without thinking, I lightly kicked the cat with the Red Ball boots I was wearing (Roy and I had each purchased a pair for the trip, but we didn't want them to look new, so we had worn them to the bridge to get a little fish slime and blood on them to hide our noviceness). The cat's fin sliced right through the boot and dug deep into my foot. I can tell you now that in terms of sudden pain, I had never been that quickly overcome with something so severe and excruciating, and I've broken and dislocated just about every bone in my body.

In panicked response, I kicked my foot to get the fish away from me. The cat went sailing through the air directly toward Roy, who had turned to my screams of pain. The fish struck Roy full-length: its tail at his chest, its head in his groin. Without a sound except for a sudden sucking of air, Roy stared at me wide-eyed in terror for a second, then dropped to the concrete, his knees sounding a sharp crack as they hit, and then fell flat forward on the bridge. I was so scared at that moment both from the intense pain that was rocketing around in my rubber boot and from the thought that I had just sent the sailcat's huge dorsal fin directly into Roy's gut and that he was lying before me dying. As I tried to ask Roy if he was okay, I glanced down at my boot which was leaking blood out of the hole that the fin had cut. A large puddle of blood was forming under my foot, and a piece of something was sticking out of the boot. I figured it to be the fin of the fish that had been torn off and left embedded in my foot. A wave of nausea crumbled me, and I grabbed the bridge railing to keep from falling and passing out.

As I stared at the blood-covered thing sticking out of my white Red Ball boot, the rest of my body turned cold and clammy. I heard a soft guttural groan come from Roy. I looked over to see him looking at the blood around my foot; he still lay face down on the concrete with his chin resting in dried scales and old bait. Our eyes momentarily met, and with a rage I have never before seen in Roy, he grumbled up at me, "I hope that fuckin' hurts," referring to the thing sticking out of my foot. I was bleeding to death, and he was glad. Apparently, the fish had not impaled him, but the cat's bony head had caught him squarely in the one spot a man does not want to be hit by anything, particularly a flying catfish. The blow (forgive me) dropped him to his knees and then some.

After Roy caught his breath and I convinced him not to throw me off the bridge, he fetched a first aid kit, removed my boot, and made me bleed out as much of the cat slime as possible. Luckily, the protruding piece was merely a part of the sock that the fin had snagged and pulled through the bloodied boot. Neither of us wanted to give up the trip to go to the hospital, so we bled the wound until such a huge amount of blood puddled on the bridge that it looked like the site of a cow butchering. We bandaged my foot, stuffed it back in the boot, and ended up paying for pin fish. At the time, none of it was funny, but I can only imagine now, as Roy and I have joked about it dozens of time since, that to the one angler who was wading below us under the bridge, the scene must have seemed very Keystone-Kop-like with a catfish flying and people dropping in its wake. By the way, in the entire three days on the boat, neither of us caught a thing until five minutes before we were to return to John's Pass when I boated a 47 pound kingfish that also attracted the attention of a large barracuda; thankfully, the mate was quick enough with the gaff to recover the fish and the tail that the 'cuda cut off.

Unfortunately, not all of my experiences with Roy left us with stories of humor. Sometimes our adventures were dangerous, and one brought us closer to dying than I care to ever be again. Since Roy's father is a military officer, Roy's dependent ID gave us access to renting boats at MacDill Air Force Base in Tampa. Since this was really our only access to boats at the time, we spent a good deal of time in the rented boats patrolling Tampa Bay for trout, reds, and snook. One early fall weekend, Roy and I had motored a small rental jon boat up Coon's Creek behind the Air Force base. In the previous weeks we'd had fairly good luck taking juvenile snook on top water plugs—particularly size four Bagley's Bang-o-lures. We spent the day drifting through Coon's Creek casting to the mangrove shoreline catching the small linesiders and some jacks and trout as well. The light current that was bringing the tide into the creek kept us drifting at such a perfect pace that we were able to work both shorelines without having to reposition the boat. I stood forward casting from the little platform on the bow, and Roy stood aft on the molded bench seat by the small outboard.

The day was close to perfect: a light breeze, warm sun, enough fish to keep us interested, and the quiet company of two good friends. We drifted through the twists and turns of the creek and congratulated each other on our catches and occasionally talked about important things of life. At the time, Roy was in a bad frame of mind. Stormy had been pregnant for about six months and he was terrified at the prospect of becoming a father. All summer, he had begged me and Rob and Jota to help him find a way to run away from all of the new responsibility. He manufactured ways of faking his own death so Stormy and the baby would have enough insurance to be comfortable. We weren't pleased with Roy's desire to run from responsibility, but we certainly understood his fear. After all, he was 24, still in school, had no money, and had huge debt; a baby was a scary thing. Besides, contriving *Mission Impossible*-like plans for hiding a friend from the world made for some fantastic fantasies. (Needless to say, Roy is a great father to two of the most beautiful little girls in the world and to Roy, the fifth, who at six months old already promises to be the best defensive end ever to play at the University of Florida.

Stormy never would listen to me and name any of the kids "Redfish Brown.")

We drifted around back in Coon's Creek that day, Roy trying to come to terms with his impending fatherhood and me trying to be as supportive as I could. Very far in the distance, we could hear the report of weapon fire at the Air Force base shooting range, and we tried to guess from the sounds what sort of weapons were being fired. But suddenly, a gunshot exploded that was not in the distance and was not at the firing range. A bullet sped between us as we stood at opposite ends of the boat. The bullet was so close that we could hear it tear the air near our ears, and when it hit the mangrove behind us, it sent wooden splinters into the water and into the boat. Roy and I looked at each other in wide-eyed fear just as the firing increased. Bullets ricocheted off the water within inches of the boat, and the mangrove branches around us exploded as more bullets tore past our heads. We both dove for the bottom of the boat, hollering at the tops of our lungs for whoever was shooting to please stop, there were people out here. Crammed as low as he could get his large frame in the back of the boat, Roy reached up and started the outboard. As the bullets smacked around us, Roy and I laughed in uncontrollable hysteria. There was no doubt that we were both terrified, but all we could do to keep calm was laugh ourselves to tears as we hollered until our throats were raw for whoever was shooting to please stop. Roy got the engine started, and driving blind, we bounced off of mangroves and sand bars at full throttle until we saw the shadows of mangroves disappear at the mouth of the creek, and we ran about a half a mile out into Tampa Bay still crouched low in the standing water at the bottom of the boat until we could barely hear the gunfire and we were certain that we were far away from the bullets.

It took us about a half an hour to stop shaking and laughing, which verged in and out of crying. After we calmed down and inspected the hull for bullet holes, we frightened ourselves to silence with the thought of what ifs. What if that first bullet had hit either of us in the head and sent our brains to feed the fish? What if one of us lay bleeding from a shattered head half in the boat, half in the water? What if I had to call Stormy and tell her that her unborn baby's father was dead? In John MacDonald's classic tales of Travis McGee, Travis mentions that "the ifs can kill you, and the never-agains can gut you." I've written about Travis' ifs and never-agains before, but in the incident at Coon's Creek, I think the ifs and never agains were bigger than either Roy or I would ever want to admit.

Roy and I are gun people; we own them, shoot them, and hunt with them. Roy has been a gun owner since he was a kid, and he is also not afraid to use them. Once, armed with a shotgun, he escorted Stormy out of the store she managed after she had caught some local punks shoplifting and they had threatened to kill her. Roy showed up to be sure that those threats remained idle. But that day on Coon's Creek, I think Roy was as terrified of guns as anyone could be. I certainly was. Even after the summer's discussions of faking Roy's death, the awakening of how real death could have been that day scared both of us to an unnerving hysteria. We never spoke of the death ruse again.

Bullets would send Roy and me scrambling for cover one other time that same year. I find it frightening that two of the three times in my life when I have been in serious danger of being shot occurred in relation to fishing. I used to have a signature line on my e-mail that read "fishing is the opposite of war." The words are from George Orwell's *Coming Up for Air*. I like those words a lot. But someone pointed out to me that fishing isn't the opposite of war; that, in fact, it is war. Fishing is an instance where we intrude into another's environment and intentionally disturb the indigenous population of that environment, often killing members of that population. Once when I was a kid fishing with my dad on a pier on the Outer Banks of North Carolina, I was removing a hook from a fish I had just landed, and the fish expelled its bowels all over me. In my childlike ways I exclaimed how gross that was, and my dad very calmly looked at me and said that the fish was afraid; that the fear of death makes creatures lose control; that dying is an extremely traumatic event. I've never forgotten that about death.

I have very little experience with death: a grandmother, a good friend, and some acquaintances, but no real experience. When I was in high school, I worked on the gas dock at Willoughby Bay Marina just inside Hampton Roads by the Chesapeake Bay Bridge Tunnel. Those were important days in my growing up and learning about boats and fishing; they are days which I write about and affect how I write about boats and fishing. On one summer day, the police boat which docked at the marina came rushing up to my dock. The police told me that they had found a man who had been missing from a Chinese work boat for several weeks. They said that the dock would be crawling with reporters in a few minutes, and they asked me to keep the reporters back. I got to act official and put my hands in the cameras and tell the reporters they couldn't be on "my" dock. I'm sure I threw in a few "no comments" and "hi moms" as well.

Just before the police transferred the body bag from the police boat to the morgue van, one of the officers asked me to jump down in the boat to help them hold the body bag open for the detectives to photograph the corpse and then to help lift the bag onto the dock. I was 16 or 17, so I thought it would be a cool thing to get to do. The experience silenced me for three days. Years later, when I fell prey to the college illusion of becoming a poet, I wrote about that experience. It was my first attempt at coming to terms with death:

4:18

the cop had been a friend.
filled his boat at my dock and
let me harass the speeders he would
ticket. we laughed together a lot.
asked me once if I could
run a mile in a minute then
pointed a gun at my feet.
we were good friends and that's why
he let me see.

the chinese man had been floating
in the bay for six days when
the cop had pulled him up.
fell off a work boat, they said.
or was pushed. lots
of reporters on my dock
that day. but the cop said
none could see. only I
was invited.

the cop unzipped
the bag and I choked
on the smell. the man's face
was swollen like a balloon with eyes
staring at nothing. I thought
he was wearing white work gloves,
but his nails told me that the color
had left his once dark skin.
blue shirt. white skin.

the chinese man was wearing
a watch that had stopped
at 4:18. stopped soon after
the man had. the bay had taken
the life of one man and one watch
at 4:18. I stared
at the two dead faces and wondered
which upset me more.

As far as poetry goes, it's not much. Only now do I see the few interesting things I tried to do: the stanzas are balanced, each beginning with the refrain "the cop" or "the chinese man." And the only capital letter in the poem is "I." I guess the poem was really more about me, the "I," and my trying to come to terms with this first encounter with death. There's a first I could have done without. I've seen a few dead bodies since then, but that experience will always haunt me. But, the day on Coon's Creek left me asking lots more questions about our mortality.

I often think now about those days of being afraid of my mortality, of coming to terms with having almost lost Roy or having been killed myself. Perhaps that's one of the reasons that relationships such as those we have with close friends, with partners, are so important. They provide not only the comfort and security and support of good friendships, but they provide an outlet through which to talk about and come to terms with the scary things in life too.

I couldn't tell you now how many times Roy and I fished together before he moved to Dallas and I to Kansas, but in many ways those days of fishing have not stopped. We subscribe to the same magazines, watch the same shows, dream the same dreams, go to boat shows and lust after the same boats. And we talk regularly; we have a long-distance fishing relationship. And though we both are not really where we want to be, we know that we will fish together again in our home waters and that we will not have to leave them. And so for now I remember the stories, the good times fishing with Roy—the big fish, the funny trips, and even the frightening experiences. Aldo Leopold wrote in *Sand County Almanac* that "There are degrees and kinds of solitude." Out here I know a certain kind of solitude, a loneliness away from friends and family and salt water. And so I spend late nights, like tonight, remembering places and people and other times, and I hammer those times into my keyboard hoping to recapture a few moments of those memories. Tonight, Roy is heavy on my mind, not just because I miss his ability to help me see things more clearly once in a while, but because tonight I miss fishing with Roy.

Sharks and Gators

In his book *Coming Up For Air*, George Orwell writes: "Fear! We swim in it. It's our element. Everyone that isn't scared stiff of losing his job is scared stiff of war, or fascism, or communism, or something."

It's an interesting thing to say that fear is our element. Orwell is certainly right; in many ways we live in fear of lots of things; in many ways we put ourselves in situations simply to experience fear: horror movies, haunted houses, bungee jumping, amusement park rides, sky diving, ABBA, and so on. But, these are examples of controlled fear; we always know there's so much of an element of safety that the fear is only superficial. In many ways we try to avoid the real fears in life. When we actually experience real fear, it often leaves us shaking and sick. Our hearts pound in our chest and we gasp for air when we think someone has broken into our home when we are jerked from sleep by a sudden noise in the night. Adrenaline rushes, sweat chills the skin, and our hands shake as we try to slowly recapture control of our breathing. I don't make any bones about it; I won't play the macho game. I hate being that kind of scared, the kind of scared when the phone rings in the middle of the night.

I remember being scared that afternoon on Coon's Creek with Roy, scared beyond being able to do anything but laugh hysterically until tears of fear leaked out of my eyes in some uncontrolled reaction to terror. I also remember being scared into a dysfunctional numbness one night in Norfolk, Virginia. I still shiver at the images in my head of one of my brothers lying face down in a parking lot, handcuffed and beaten. His wrist broken, and his screams for help and of pain unheeded by the 30 or so people standing, watching the scene. My other brother was hidden nearby watching, scared, and I could feel his presence as I raised my hands in a non-aggressive gesture of compliance and passivism to the man standing before me with a gun in his outstretched arms pointed directly at my face. The same man who had moments before beaten each of my brothers; first Ben with a billy club and then Adam as he lay handcuffed on the ground as Ben ran for safety. I looked directly into the gun's barrel expecting a flash, an explosion. I was too numb to shake or cry or panic or even wet myself. The man holding the gun had put the cold barrel right to my forehead, looked me square in face, and calmly told me, "You are now going to die, motherfucker."

He had said it so matter-of-factly that I instantly believed it, and my mind blurred out the rest of the world. I felt nothing. Kurt Vonnegut's words in *Slaughterhouse Five* seem appropriately relevant: "How nice to feel nothing, and still get full credit for being alive." I suppose I was fully alive, though I felt nothing of it. I couldn't hear the noises of the crowd that gathered and watched from a safe distance, the screams of my brother in pain to my right, the approaching sirens. I just stared into that barrel and waited, wondering if I would see anything in the instant between the bullet leaving the barrel and it hitting me in the head. But I never found out, as the gunman ordered me to the ground, like he had ordered my brother to the ground before he cuffed his hands behind his back and lifted him by the cuffs, cracking his wrist. In those moments, before my other brother turned a garden hose on the surreal scene, before the cops finally arrived, before I calmed myself from the resolve that I was going to die, in those moments, I felt total fear.

Zane Grey wrote that "fishing is a condition of mind wherein you cannot possibly have a bad time." While I'm sure those of us who have been seasick, frozen, hungry, mosquito eaten, lost, or otherwise miserably uncomfortable might want to argue the finer points of Grey's claim, Grey does not say that we can't be scared when we fish. I find what scares us interesting and that what scares us is what we are taught to fear. With the possible exception of falling, we are born unafraid. I don't claim to be an expert on phobias, but my understanding is that we must learn to be afraid. Babies will play with snakes, guns, or fire with little fear. But teach the same child to fear a snake, and even a quick glimpse of a crooked stick lying in a path might evoke images of a cottonmouth lying there and send a cool sweat to the skin, a tight feeling in the chest, a rush of nervous adrenaline to a shaking body.

We learn fear; sometimes silly fear. For instance, the *Jaws* movies created such an awful image of sharks that I now know people who grew up in the Midwest who claim to be certain that there's a shark stalking them when they're in the deep end of the community swimming pool. In fact, there's a woman where I work who upon her first visit to the Gulf of Mexico refused to enter the water deeper than her ankles because she was certain there were man-eating great whites the size of Greyhound busses cruising the knee-deep water, looking for tasty morsels of Midwesterner. I know that in some places along the Gulf she might have had the opportunity to wade for miles in ankle deep shallows and still enjoy the green gulf water, but to restrict one's self from a few more feet of water because of the memory of a rubber shark seemed laughable to me. I found this fear so silly that I felt obligated to weave a few yarns about the dreaded ankle sharks of the Gulf which live in the sand below the surf. On her next visit, she never even got her feet wet.

I grew up with sharks. Well that's not exactly true since I really grew up with my brothers, but there were times I would have preferred sharks. Because my family spent so much time on the water, sharks were just a natural part of the surrounding; I learned respect for these beautiful animals, not fear. I remember standing on the beach in Kitty Hawk, North Carolina, one summer watching my mother Boogie Board in the surf. During Outer Banks summers, the warm, blue-green surf is always filled with life: tandem-jumping porpoises, cruising rays, bluefish, turtles, sharks. So, seeing an animal in the water with you was no big deal. I had pulled big sand tigers to the piers all over the Outer Banks, and my dad and I used to have a blast catching small sharks and dogfish from the beach using sandfleas as bait before shark populations diminished due to uncontrolled netting and poor conservation practices. But on the day I watched my mom frolicking in the waves, I caught a glimpse of a sight that will forever remind me of just how much a part of the surf sharks are.

Mom had caught a nice clean wave and was riding back to shore (yes, Mom rides waves). She was laughing and having an all-around good time. That summer, the water was particularly clean and it glistened emerald green in the afternoon sun. The wave took form, building to crest, dropping to trough. As it did, six dark shadows appeared in the wave with

Mom, three on either side of her. The wave started to curl back toward the surface from which it had risen, and her flanking company pushed their dorsal fins through the surface. Each shark was only about four feet long, but there were six of them riding the wave with Mom. I had no idea what to do or say, but when I looked into her face, I watched her look left then right and then smile her own toothy grin. She rode the white water surf all the way to shore, and came on to the beach shouting excitedly, "Did you see that? Did you see that?" She tells this story much better than I ever could, but then again, she had a front row seat.

In our times on the Outer Banks and in Florida, our family developed a simple respect for sharks. They were part of the world into which we intruded when we broke the surface of the water. They belonged there; we were trespassing. If my brothers are surfing or another family member is swimming, we have a simple rule: if someone on shore calls you in, you come—no questions. If you're on shore and see a shark, you call the others in, but you do it calmly. There's no need to induce panic or fear. People react badly when scared, and that's when things go wrong. Sometimes, if the swimmer or surfer is far enough away from the beach we'll cut the air with our hand mimicking a fin or give the divers' hand signal for shark. It's certainly not a sign you want to see if you're out deep, but it lets you know to keep your eyes alert or to head for shore with diligence and without panicking.

Tourists don't react the same way. I suppose it's a matter of familiarity, but there are extremes. I was swimming at the north beach of Virginia Beach one summer when a pod of porpoises came into the surf. In a flash of white water and screams, the tourists fled the water. I paddled around quite peacefully until the screams from the shore of "fins!" and "sharks!" just got to be a bit too much. I paddled in and considered telling the crowd that those were just porpoises, but I figured it'd keep more tourists away from the beach if rumors of shark-infested waters and crazy locals spread back to Ohio.

Growing up with this kind of familiarity of sharks and knowing that they are around gives an interesting perspective. A few summers ago, I was down at Sugar Loaf Key, Florida—where I often roam—with some friends who had ventured down from Tampa. Late one afternoon my friends Todd, Raul, and Tom and I decided to explore the back country and work the flats for a while. We had hoped to tangle with a cobia or permit, but our plans were disrupted when a tremendous squall pinned us on the flats for hours. We couldn't see the oyster bars or reasonably navigate back through the channels—and, okay, I'll admit it, we weren't exactly certain which mangrove-lined channel was the right one to take back—so we anchored the 18-foot Carolina Skiff to ride out the rain. As we sat there, we noticed lots of fair-sized sharks cruising the skinny water around us. The wind had picked up so much that the bimini top we had put up to keep the rain off was catching all of the wind and dragging our small five-pound mushroom anchor across the flats. To keep the boat from sailing into the mangroves, the other three members of the crew jumped into the water to push it back out. It turned out that the warm Key water was much more comfortable than the driving rain and wind so we all lay down on a sandbar and held the boat fast against the storm.

After several hours of relentless downpour, the sun, hidden by clouds, started to drop out into the Gulf and the back country started to hide in the shadows of a rainy evening. We figured that we should try to make our way back before the tropical darkness hid all of the channels from our view. With Raul and Tom joining me back in the boat, Todd took hold of the bow line and started to pull us back toward a channel. As he pulled us along, I caught a glimpse of a dark movement several yards ahead of him. Two large black tips were cruising right at him, and I calmly announced, "Todd get in the boat." Had I said the same thing to either of my brothers, they would have simply climbed aboard without hesitation or question. Todd, however, turned and looked at me inquisitively. The sharks had cut the distance between themselves and Todd in half and were still on a zig-zagged collision course. The other two on the boat saw the black tips at about this time, and I could see that there was soon going to be some unproductive screaming so I tried again. This time, with as much calmed authority as I could muster I told Todd to get in the boat immediately. I guess he could sense the urgency in my voice or he remembered the numbers of sharks we had seen that day, because in one diving leap he came head first across the bow and belly flopped onto the forward deck. No panic, but enough fear to have sent him aerial onto the deck.

My mom and I argue a lot about the difference between risk and being stupid. She thinks a lot of what I do is carelessly stupid. I think some things involve a little risk; and, I like adventure. I'm also intrigued by the notion of risk. John D. MacDonald writes about risk in *The Dreadful Lemon Sky* in terms of a "risk-reward ratio." That is, at what point do the dangers of a risk exceed the reward. I like to think of risk that way. I guess we all do; we all ask, "Is it worth it?"

I remember distinctly the first time I heard the word *risk*. I was probably about four, and we were living in Tallahassee at the time. I was playing with my childhood friend Marc Austin in a fort/playhouse that his parents had built in the backyard. The fort was raised two or three feet off the ground on pilings to give it a sort of tree-house effect. Marc and I were engaged in some deeply important adventure that had placed us in a situation of having to jump from the fort if we were going to manage to save the world. It was one of those adventures that adults would have never noticed was occurring, but we knew for certain that the fate of human kind depended on us completing our mission. I think a lot of adults forget how many times kids save the world each day in backyards, empty lots, and couch-cushion forts; I think on some days we need to remember. We stood teetering on the edge of the small deck that surrounded the fort, swords in hand. "Do we risk it?" Marc asked just before we jumped. "Yeah, we risk it," came my reply, captivated by the word I'd never heard.

It was just the word I needed. Suddenly I had a term that described that feeling of possible peril, of chance, of probable hazard that had to be overcome to reach reward. I knew and loved the feeling; now I had a word and I could name the thing. Now I knew what climbing just one more branch up was; now I knew what swinging just a little higher was. All afternoon, my four-year-old chatter was ripe with the word as we leapt and climbed and rescued and defended: "Let's risk it!" "Is there a risk?" "Should we take the risk?" Not only did I need that word somehow, but the very sound of it felt comfortable in my mouth. It rolled out in sentence after sentence until I was sure Marc had to be wondering why I insisted on inserting it into every concoction of words that dripped out of my mouth. Thankfully, four-year-olds aren't that critical of their peers' language yet, and I took the afternoon to make a new word into a friend.

Now, let me be clear: I do like risk. But my notion of risk is probably a little different than some people's. I like to be out in the thick of the world: hiking, climbing, rafting, kayaking, canoeing, and I like to be away from people when I do those things. Sure, a friend or a small group is fine, but I like the sensation of being away from help. I like knowing that if anything goes wrong—and it could at any moment—that it's up to me to live through it. It's a simple survival fantasy, I suppose. But, I don't like the extreme to which some take that feeling. You won't find me bungee jumping or base jumping, nor will you find me climbing a thousand-foot rock face without ropes—unless it's absolutely necessary. That is, I don't take Chris-McCandless-caliber risks; if I walk into a place, I'm going to be sure I am prepared to walk out. I'm convinced that most of the time Mom's just being paranoid and overly worried about her sons' risks, but sometimes (rarely, Mom) she's right.

When Roy and I were living in Tampa, we regularly fished an area of the bay known as the clam bar. The clam bar is easy to find: if you drive south on 275, just before you cross the Sunshine Skyway, look east and you'll see a definitive white sandbar that runs parallel to the shore and then bends east for a mile or so into the bay. That's the clam bar. If you know the water, you can wade the quarter of a mile or so out to the clam bar without ever getting your hips wet. It took us a few tries before we "knew the water," and sometimes we'd end up swimming while holding our rods in our teeth. Roy and I liked fishing the clam bar because it held fish, but also because despite being very visible, very few people fished it (until Frank Seargent wrote about it in the *Tampa Tribune*).

When Roy left Tampa for Dallas, he made me promise not to wade the clam bar alone. We agreed that it was just too dangerous to be a mile or so away from shore, in the water, with no way to contact anyone. Mom insisted that I take Roy's advice, so I agreed not to fish the bar solo. But by the summer, I had to break that promise.

Early one morning, long before sunrise, I drove out 275 and took the exit to our access to the clam bar. I knew the routine by heart. I pulled off the main road onto a small service road and followed it until the fence surrounding the bridge construction site prevented me from going any farther. I unloaded my gear and inflated the small rubber boat we had purchased to drag out and anchor that held coolers with lunch and spare tackle—it was a big raft. I put on my wading shoes, and with a brisk breeze blowing into my face, I headed into the water before the sky was even pink with hints of the coming sun. With the boat holding my gear in tow, I made my way into hip deep water thinking the tide must be at full high. The wind lapped water at my waist, and I strained to make out anything in the darkness. I knew that I had about a 20 minute walk before I would feel the grassy bottom give way to the sandy bottom and my knees would rise inches above the choppy water. Gulls screamed in the darkness and faint splashes whispered that there were feeding fish around.

After about 20 minutes of wading and dragging the raft, the bottom started to slip away below me, and I found myself in chest deep water. I pulled the raft along side of me and draped an arm over its inflated gunwales. I knew I had to be close and that I must have just taken an odd angle in the darkness, but that if I just kept walking I had to find the bar sooner than later. I pressed on, using the raft for support in the light choppy water. For the next 20 minutes or so the bottom would rise, giving me encouraged relief that I was finally on the bar, and then would drop away again, causing me to wonder if I had misgauged how long I had been walking. I was certain that I was in the right place since I had parked where we always parked and entered the water where we always entered the water. But as the greys of dawn started playing shadow games with my eyes, I found myself clinging to the raft in water that was well over my head.

When the morning sun finally began to puddle the water in golden pink light, I caught a silhouetted glimpse of small waves crashing on the clam bar—several hundred yards to my left. I was paddling around in the main channel in the dark. I made a beeline for the sandy shallow water and when my feet finally rested on the white sand I realized what had happened. The construction site fence had been moved a mile or so south in the three or four months since I had been there, and I had entered the water well beyond where the clam bar bends east into the bay. I had been walking parallel to the bar and ended up in the channel. My heart and mind did a quick what-if panic regarding morning boat traffic; thank somebody that I could fish on weekdays and avoid weekend boat traffic. I was glad Roy and I also had made a rule about fishing on weekends: we didn't do it in Tampa; accessible areas were just too damn crowded.

After I sucked in a few gulps of morning salt air, I shrugged at myself and decided not to waste the trip; I'd just be more careful the next time. I anchored the raft and rigged a light spinning outfit with a Zaraspook. I love topwater fishing, particularly on the flats. When redfish, trout, snook, or even jacks slam a topwater plug, there's nothing like it. I stood casting into the wind to work the grass flats on the outside of the bar. The head wind made casting difficult, particularly with the wind grabbing the bulky Zaraspook and pushing it back against my casting intentions.

The choppy water made me reconsider the effectiveness of the topwater artificial, and I wandered back to the raft to switch to a gold spoon. The sun had taken center stage and hung in full glow above the horizon. I put on sun glasses and reached for a satchel of spoons. As I did, movement out of the corner of my right eye caught my attention. A dark shadow was distinctly visible against the white sand of the bar. The shadow had crept out of the dark green grass on the other side of the sandbar and was now starkly visible against the white bottom. A hammerhead of about six feet was lazily zigzagging around the bar examining the sand for morsels of a morning meal. It wasn't necessarily a big hammerhead, but six feet was plenty big if it was a hammerhead. They are very aggressive, and I put the raft between me and it. I knew that the raft was little protection, so I slid my knife into my right hand and held my light spinning outfit in the left, as though that offered any more protection than a tiny bit of peace of mind. The shark hadn't seen me and certainly wasn't reacting to my presence, but I was reacting to it and wishing the shore wasn't so damn far away.

When the shark moved in to what was just too close for me I decided to try to frighten it away. I took an oversized plug from the satchel and threw it. The plug crashed into the water just above the shark's head, and the hammerhead churned, startled, turned tail in a thumping splash, and dashed back into the shadows of the grass flats. I blew out the lungs of air I had been clenching in my chest. "Okay," I deliberately told myself, "I need to be a bit more aware today. I'm alone, and the warm summer water has brought a lot of animals to the flats." But I stayed close to the raft and cast from there with the sheath to my knife unsnapped and handy. I knew I was scared, but I tried to rationalize: just one shark; it was more scared than I was; I can handle this; I heard fish jumping. So my eyes leapt to every shadow in the choppy water as I cast aimlessly about the flats.

I probably should have left then, but I didn't. I kept reassuring myself that everything was fine, that I, of all people, could handle being scared while fishing. I also told myself that I wasn't about to be frightened away from a day's fishing by a shark. As I deliberately laughed at myself, I forced myself to regain a bit of confidence. I let go of the raft, and with each cast, I made myself take another step away from the safety of the flimsy inflated boat toward the grass flats where the trout and redfish had to be waiting for me, where the shark had disappeared into the darkness. My breathing became more regular and I tried to force myself into the zone where fishermen lose themselves, where casting becomes an involuntary motion, where dreams dance in the wind, and nothing else in the world can intrude into one's mind—the real reason we fish. But forcing one's self into this zone just doesn't work. Despite my effort, my eyes jumped to every shadow they caught glimpse of, and each time my glands shot another dose of adrenaline into my blood stream.

I knew it was probably not worth trying to fish when I was that jumpy, but my stupid self-pride wouldn't let me leave. My arms kept casting the weedless gold spoon into the water around me, but my eyes paid more attention to scanning the waters for movement. I'm glad they did. About a half-hour after I vanquished the hammerhead back to the depths, my nervous eyes again caught movement on the sandbar. This time the shadows were smaller, but there were five of them. I walked briskly back to the boat, reeling the gold spoon back in, praying nothing hit it this time—it's not often a fisherman actually prays, "Dear God, please don't let a fish hit my lure," but I didn't want a wounded, splashing fish anywhere near me.

Part of my fear grew from the fact that these shadows were not lazily cruising the sandbar as the hammerhead had been; these dark figures were jittery and headed right toward me and the boat. When the sharks got about 25 feet from the boat, which I had placed between me and them, they split up. Three moved quickly to my right, two to my left. They passed outside of me and the boat and I turned to watch the group of three pass by. Black tips. All about three or four feet long, but they were definitely black tips. I started to sigh as they passed by, as if avoiding me, but once they did get past, the three on the right turned frantically and headed straight for me. I had lost sight of the two others.

Now, as I have said, I am not really afraid of sharks *per se*, but I will confess that at that moment I was really scared. I smashed the rod down on the surface of the water, trying to scare the three off, but the splash only momentarily deterred them. The three passed so close to my legs, inspecting, that one bumped the anchor line and momentarily panicked, sending water spraying into the air, across the bow, and onto my chest as it slapped its tail in the shallow water. Just as the three got about 10 feet past me they turned for another pass, and the other two joined in at their side. In obviously nervous fashion, they headed right at me. Not knowing what else to do, I jumped into the boat spilling tackle boxes and generally disrupting all of the tackle I had so methodically packed the night before. The boat wasn't exactly big enough for me and the tackle, so as I sat on it I had to be careful not to move too suddenly for fear of tipping the raft. I was also worried that some of the spilled lures might find their way to puncturing the raft. Gingerly I reached to the bow to pull the anchor line in.

Luckily, the on-shore breeze and the incoming tide began slowly moving the raft toward the shore. I was too scared to dangle my hands or legs over and afraid to move too much, so I sat cramped in the raft. The wind slowly pushed me toward shore, but the what-ifs were playing havoc with my mind and I wanted solid ground under my feet. I carefully took off my shirt and held it up, hoping it would act as a sail and increase my speed; it didn't. It took me close to an hour to drift back in and at least two hours to put all of my lures back in their appropriate spaces in my satchels and boxes. I tried to laugh at myself for being silly and overreacting, and as I drove home, I constructed the story I'd tell my friends about the "shark attack." When I did finally tell the story that afternoon, it was over the phone to Captain Gregg Gentile of Treasure Coast Guide Service, who would give me fishing reports for my column in *The Fisherman* magazine once a week. Captain Gentile listened to my heroic telling and then told me, "Sid, one day you're going to end up a grease spot on the water."

Sharks are one thing, gators are another. I have always been afraid of gators in ways that I could never be afraid of sharks. I guess part of that comes from not really being familiar with gators. I've certainly been around them since I was a little kid, but I never learned about them like I learned about sharks. Maybe if the Discovery channel would have a "Gator Week" to go along with Shark week, I'd learn enough to calm some of the fear. But my fear of gators goes beyond simple fear of the unknown; there's something very primal about it. I don't avoid gators. In fact, because I'm afraid of them, I try to get out to watch them as often as possible. When I first moved to Tampa, I'd spend countless days wandering along and paddling around the Hillsborough River and local lakes just watching these reptiles. I would sit for hours watching their motionless bodies, staring into those cold black eyes through binoculars thinking, "these things are just too primitive." My roommate at the time bought me a replica of a yellow street sign that read "caution gator crossing"; it still hangs in my office.

I was so intrigued by gators that I'd take my friends who would visit out to see them; I learned where the big ones were likely to be. Once, when an old girlfriend was visiting, I took her to see gators. In my boastful confidence, I went tramping through a muddy, swampy area of the Hillsborough. She was less eager to be milling around in the mosquitos and cypress knees and was trailing many yards behind as I hollered encouragements for her to catch up. In my careless romping through the muck, my booted foot came down square on top of a gator. It was a small one, about three and a half feet long, and my boot came to rest just behind its head on its shoulders. The thing whipped its tail and tried to pull free in a hissing grunt. Its retreat would have sent me sprawling into the mud, belly down into its world, had I not been holding onto a branch above my head to steady myself against the ankle-breaking cypress knees in the soggy bottom. I was able to keep from falling, and in my panic I half jumped, half did a pull up and ended up pulling myself as far up the branch as I could. I must have also shouted in panic because as the little gator rapidly headed for the safety of the river, I could hear my date scrambling back the way we came.

I try to kid myself once in a while that I'm not afraid of gators, but that's usually a short-lived joke. After all, when we were kids, Dad and Mom used to let us feed the gators marshmallows at Alligator Point near Tallahassee; I really shouldn't be afraid of these things. But I am.

Luckily, I'm in better control of my fear some times than others. My friend Rob and I had gone fishing one afternoon on the Hillsborough when I realized how jumpy some people can be (Rob is the most jumpy person in the wild that I've ever known, and he'd be the first to admit it). Rob and I were paddling a canoe down the Hillsborough up near Tampa Palms and Lutz and casting small bass lures hoping that the river would take the opportunity to teach us a little about bass fishing. I had become so frustrated with the lousy casting action and poor drag of a cheap microlight outfit I was carrying that in my anger with it, I tossed it to the bank. Rob, trying to calm me, paddled over to the shore to retrieve the outfit knowing I'd later be angry if I just left it in the woods. After retrieving the rod and reel, Rob placed the flat of his paddle against an overhanging tree to push us back away from the shore. I was still frustrated and angry, and as I turned to see just what the hell Rob was doing back there, I noticed that he had managed to pin a water moccasin to the tree with his paddle. Rob was completely unaware that he had the snake trapped, so I asked in my still angry voice, "You gonna let that thing in the boat with us?" and I gestured with my eyes to the end of his paddle. Rob followed my gaze and the instant he saw the snake whipping in panic, trying to get free, he let out a shriek that was more annoying than the possibility of sharing a canoe with a pissed-off moccasin. His reaction also made him retract the paddle, freeing the snake. Thankfully, he managed to push the canoe just far enough away from the bank that the spasming snake dropped outside the boat and we were able to paddle away before the thing decided to take revenge, as I've seen moccasins do before. Needless to say, Rob was jittery, and I was content in my anger.

We paddled on down river and after a few minutes of distance from that annoying microlight, I decided to work a bed of lily pads with a weedless mouse. We worked the canoe past a few big gators and found a quiet spot to cast into the weeds. The carp were in mating season, so an occasional splash disrupted the surface, but for the most part the water was calm and the three or four gators we had passed simply sat soaking in the sun. The damn rod and reel still managed to give me trouble, but Rob and I fell into quiet conversation, and I sat in the bow taking in the comfort of the day, occasionally laughing at the moccasin incident.

As I sat, becoming less and less angry and more and more content with the day, I heard a carp roll and splash just to the port side of the canoe. In the moment after the splash, the canoe lurched starboard and Rob started shrieking again. I turned my head just enough to see Rob beginning to stand and look to the water as though he were going to jump. I grabbed for the gunwales to steady the canoe and hollered, "What the hell are you doing?!?" His shriek response came, "I'm getting the hell out of here! That gator's too damn close!" In my most authoritative voice, I ordered him to sit down and I tightened my grip on the gunwales to steady against his jumpy movements. When I asked him again what he was doing, he said he thought the splash was a gator and he didn't want to be in the canoe with a gator that close. It took me a while to get him to understand that the splash had been a carp and that even if it had been a gator, it probably wasn't a good idea to jump into the water with it.

I guess that level of fear, the fear that one's about to be mauled by a Florida gator, will certainly cause some panic reactions; I'm just glad mine are a bit more controlled, since I seem to end up chasing my fears more frequently than Rob, and since I really didn't want to take a swim in the Hillsborough. I laughed at him for hours that afternoon; he ended up laughing about it too. I've laughed at him about it every chance I can get; in fact, I'm laughing about it right now. Rob is getting married next month; I'll probably work the story into my toast.

Rob was with me and Roy, or should I say, I was with Roy and Rob when I had my closest encounter with a gator. The two of them were waiting for me one afternoon when I finished teaching my course at the University of South Florida with news of a nearby lake that held bass. We had promised

Stormy that we'd find a place closer to home to fish since our daily drives to St. Petersburg or Homosassa or other Gulf costal waters kept Roy away from home more than he should have been. So, we had started scouting lakes within a 10-mile radius of our homes. On this particular day Roy and Rob seemed confident that they had found *the* lake.

Now, as I've mentioned in earlier chapters, I really don't know that much about freshwater fishing, particularly bass fishing, but fishing mere minutes from my door had an appeal. So the three of us headed out to the lake. When we got there, rods, reels, tackle in hand, Roy and Rob led me along a sand path for about a half mile to a small lake that was hidden in the Florida vegetation. We walked down to a marshy bank and the two of them, grinning ear to ear, pointed at the bank and announced, "That's it; we just wade in right there." From the end of the path I surveyed the spot to which they were pointing and announced right back at them, "I am not about to wade in there; that's a 13-foot gator." I pointed to a damn big gator lying just to left of where they were suggesting we wade. I wish I could have photographed the fear in their faces as they explained to me that they had been wading there just the day before. I just shook my head and snickered at them.

As they sat swallowing their fear and trying to tell me that it really was worth fishing, the megagator decided to leave the bank and head into the lake. Its sun-greyed hide slipped into the brown lake and its huge dragon-like tail pushed the big reptile out into the water. When it was about 15 feet from the bank, a big chunk of the bank followed the gator out into the water. Roy and Rob and I looked quizzically at each other trying to figure out why this big piece of dirt and grass and marsh was chasing the gator. As we stood there proverbially scratching our heads a voice said to us "Oh, you found him. Good; keep an eye on him." We turned to see a park ranger standing behind us. The ranger explained that they had been removing the gators from this chain of lakes since so many people made recreational use of them. This big gator had been removed once before but found its way back and had eluded them for several months. They had set baits and hooked the beast, but because it was so big, the gator had simply pulled the line and the ground to which it was staked. The ranger asked us to keep an eye on the small floating island while he went to call the official gator remover. So, we did.

When the gator hunter finally arrived in a pickup truck with a small aluminum jon boat, he told the ranger he'd need all of our help on this one. Rob and Roy and I eagerly agreed to volunteer, since gator removal seemed a deeply cool masculine thing to spend an afternoon doing. We tossed our bassing equipment to the grass and helped the gator guy put his jon boat in the water. The official gator hunter motored the green aluminum hull out to the floating island. The gator dove for the bottom when the jon boat approached. The ranger rode out in the boat with the hunter, and he took hold of the stake and freed it from the marshy island. With the big metal stake in hand, the ranger sat on the forward bench facing the stern, his feet planted wide and firm against the center bench. Grasping the stake like a water ski tow rope with the line trailing off behind the boat and into the dark lake waters, he nodded to the hunter, who gave the 15 horsepower engine enough gas until the rope went tight and the battle began.

The gator did not come up, but the small engine slowly dragged the boat, the two men, the stake and line, and the gator toward us on the shore. The engine whined and revved as the man at the throttle opened it as wide as possible. The gator stayed deep, pulling against the engine in a tug of war. Eventually, the small motor won out and the bow of the boat came to the grass where Roy and Rob grabbed it and pulled it ashore. The ranger, wearied from his struggle with the leashed gator, handed me the stake and I leaned back keeping the line tight. It was at this moment that the gator decided to come up, and he did so rather furiously. He was rolling and splashing in the shallow waters near the shore as I handed the stake over to the official hunter. In the moments I had held the rope, I felt real strength pulling at the other end, pulling at the hook buried deep in its jaw. Somewhere at the other end of that line was an angry reptile that was not having the conscious thoughts that I was having, not considering what was happening in any spiritual, metaphysical, or even cool masculine way. It was operating in a pure instinctive drive to stay alive. It resisted threat with all of its muscle, all of its being; it knew nothing else. And, that frightened me. I was glad to give up the tether that momentarily linked me to that sort of primitive thought.

Pulling on the line that was hooked in the gator's jaw, the hunter backed up until the monster was thrashing about on solid land. He handed his end of the line to the ranger before taking a long pole with a loop of rope at one end and fastened a new, stronger link of rope around its jaws. He then carefully worked his way to the rear of the animal and tied another line around its massive tail. With the two ropes pulling in opposite directions, the gator could only roll over and over, spinning the ropes in our hands. But when the gator finally ceased its frantic rolling, the hunter stepped up to the reptile's head, grabbed its snout, and wound an entire roll of duct tape around its jaws to keep its mouth closed. He then told us to hold the gator down and to keep the tail secure. The ranger and Rob pulled the tail line taut and I climbed on top, placing my hands behind its head trying to pin its shoulders to the ground.

I could feel the strength in its shoulders as it tried to resist my weight on top of it and pull against the line holding its tail secure. The smell of wild animal rose off of its rough back and haunted the backs of my nostrils. From my position above its head, I could look into its eyes. There was no fear there; it did not blink nor did its eyes seem to beg mercy. The animal just lay there, all muscles flexed and tense, but with little or no movement. In its eyes I saw everything people like to believe they are not. This animal simply sat and waited to feel any slack in the line, any give in the tape that held its jaws, any relaxation in my pressure. And I knew that if it found that brief weakness it would turn and slash me or Roy or Rob or the Ranger or even the professional gator hunter into chunks of useless meat and fragmented bones without the slightest bit of thought or remorse. It would preserve itself at all costs.

I think that moment of contact with those empty eyes taught me more than ever that we cannot anthropomorphize animals. The countless numbers of times people have asked me how I can hurt fish or shoot animals or even stand to hurt a shrimp when hooking it as bait has always left me frustrated. I try to be a humane person; I don't want to inflict pain. But the human qualities of pain and fear and love and all of the other emotions that we attribute to animals simply do not exist there in the ways they do in humans. I cannot, after looking into that gator's eyes, ever think of an animal as operating on the same system of thought and emotion as people. Don't get me wrong, I certainly believe that animals think; I even admit that there are very intelligent animals like dogs, pigs, porpoises, apes—those to who we often ascribe human-like qualities of communication, loyalty, sadness—but I more readily believe that we look to see these traits in animals. Animals do feel pain; they do think. But, when we anthropomorphize those emotions in animals, we do a disservice to them by discrediting their own existence and reconstructing those lives in relationship to ours'. We wish to think of porpoise communication in terms of human communication, dog loyalty and love in terms of human love. Hell, we even name our dogs like family, treat them like family, and certainly on some level they are integral parts of our lives, but to attribute human thought and emotion to animals is simply false logic.

I must have become rather lost in the eyes of the gator because I was not aware of what was going on with the rest of the hunting party. Suddenly Roy grabbed me by the back of the collar and yanked me off of the gator with a commanding "Look out!" As he did, a long metal pole passed over my shoulder toward the gator's head. In the same instant that Roy yanked me back, the end of the pole jammed down between the gator's eyes and exploded. It was a bang stick loaded with a substantial charge, and the official gator hunter fired the load down into the primitive brain of the reptile. The animal spasmed and the tail strained against the rope as blood poured from its head covering the black eyes which still had not changed focus or even blinked. We watched the gator for about 45 minutes before the hunter decided it was safe to transport the animal to the back of his truck. The five of us lifted the massive animal and put him in the back of the white pickup. Once there, the gator took one more thrashing attempt at winning its freedom. The bed of the truck, stained with the blood of gators past, got a new speckling of blood that ran down the beveled troughs, under the tailgate, and dripped deep crimson onto the dusty Florida grass.

In the time that we stood watching the gator die, not much was said. I remember being a little angry since I had figured that this gator would just be relocated like the rest. I didn't see the need to kill the animal. But the ranger explained that the hunter's fee was to be able to take the gator to market, and since this one had already returned once after relocation, there seemed little other option. That summer the state of Florida had increased the numbers of gators that licenced hunters could kill and sell since the populations had grown and they were intruding into human space. Intruding into human space; becoming a hazard for the millions of people who had flocked to Florida to pave over the irritating sand and swamp and to build comfortable cubed concrete condos. Boy do we have a screwed-up notion of intrusion. My father is fond of asking people who complain about gators, "How many people have been hurt by gators in the past ten years?

How many gators have been hurt by people in the same time?" It's good logic.

With the gator gone and a few more hours before any of us had to be anywhere, we waded out into the lake to catch a few bass. We stood close to each other casting to the center of the lake. Occasionally, I would take the tip of my rod and lightly brush against the backs of Rob's legs. He would, of course, shriek and splash in instant terror. But unlike most people who would catch on after the tenth time or so, Rob reacted just as jumpily after the thirtieth and fortieth time. Roy and I told him to get over it, but Rob made it plain for us: "The one time I reach my hand back to brush away your rod," he said matter-o-factly, "that'll be the one time you're not screwing with me and it will really be a gator or snake. So go on and laugh all you want, but I'm going to jump every time you do it." And, each of the hundreds of times I poked him, he did.

Reds

I've kept up my subscriptions to about a half dozen fishing magazines while I've been landlocked here in Kansas. They help to frustrate me and remind me of what I've been missing. It's a fairly inexpensive form of self-torture, but I figure if the monks could wear those scratchy robes without any skivvies to remind them of the suffering their god went through, then I can torture myself with longings for blue water in order to remind myself of what I'm missing. Between the photos in the magazines and television's airing of *Mark Sosin's Salt Water Journal*, Flip's *Walker's Cay Chronicles*, and a few other saltwater fishing shows, I manage to find plenty of time to watch other people catch saltwater fish. I try to reserve my Saturday mornings for yelling my jealousies at anglers on the television as part of my weekly hang-over cure. With magazines strewn about the floor, I flip channels between shows and flip pages between articles.

Vic Dunaway, one of the most prolific writers about salt-water angling and one of my favorite fishing magazine authors, wrote in the November 1996 issue of *Florida Sportsman*: "Every angler has his own idea about which species is the gamest. In my view, there isn't any contest. It's the redfish." He goes on to say that "All good fish will keep you guessing, but redfish seem to keep themselves guessing too. The tricks they play and the performances they put on always seem spontaneous—as much a surprise to the redfish as to you." Vic Dunaway knows his shit. I will here and now proclaim with hand on heart that if I were ever condemned to fish for only one species of fish for the rest of my life, I would plead with the judge and jury that the species be redfish. I would also most likely be charged and sentenced for murder of who ever denied me a future with sailfish and dolphin and tarpon and snook, but if forced, I could be content with a life of reds.

I've often wondered why the redfish has never earned a treatise of its own, a *Moby Dick-* or *Old Man and the Sea-*caliber book. Trout, marlin, tarpon, even bluefish have each had beautiful books written about them, extolling their beauty and prowess, but not the redfish. A few years ago I went to see the movie *Reds*, hoping that some cinematic genius had produced an epic about these Cadillacs of fish. Boy, was I disappointed. I've had similar disappointments when I found out that *The Big Red One* was not about Mark Hamill and Lee Marvin catching a really big redfish (though killing Nazis is certainly an honor-able sport), nor was *Red Dawn* about catching reds in the morning. *Red Sonya* was not as disappointing because there was at least a woman running around in her underwear with a really big sword. I didn't even bother with *Hunt for Red October*.

Someone with more sense of the poetic than I needs to wax philosophic about the redfish in a tome to be forever treasured. There need to be chapters devoted to the deep auburn color of the fish, to the wonder of its distinct black-dotted tail, to the rubbery charm of its down-turned mouth, to the strength of its big broad shoulders, and to the delicate taste of its flesh which Cajun chef Paul Prudhomme made popular with his now famous blackened redfish. Someone needs to write a book about this fish, someone who can find less sexual ways of describing it than I just did; I am, apparently, a pathetic, lonely man.

The redfish travels under many names: reds, channel bass, spottail bass, to name a few. My grandfather calls them red drum, as do many, and I've even heard them called red horses. The small ones are even known as "rats." According to what I've read about them, they're called *Sciaenops ocellatus* in Latin, even though there's never been a redfish anywhere near Rome nor a Latin speaking Roman anywhere near the south Atlantic and Gulf of Mexico where the redfish live.

I've been lucky in my catching of redfish; I've caught them in varying ways, of varying sizes, and in various locales. Like I said, these are the fish I would be content pursuing solely. Perhaps this is simply because they can be taken in so many ways and in so many places. Approaches to catching reds range from bottom rigs with cut bait to Carolina rigs with blue crabs for bait to live pin fish to gold spoons to topwater plugs to jigs to flies. I've caught them in at least as many ways as I have any other fish. But let me not try to recount each redfish; doing so would be as arrogant as boasting names and quantities of lovers (I've had more redfish). But let me remember a few of the more standout redfish I've encountered.

Like most anglers, I certainly crave catching big fish. And while really big redfish are known to prowl the Outer Banks of North Carolina in herds that turn the water red and in Florida's Indian River and Mosquito Lagoon to the tune of several world records, I will insist that Sebastian Inlet holds some of the biggest reds I've ever seen and provides an interesting challenge in catching them. Sebastian Inlet, just south of Melbourne, Florida, is home to perhaps my all-time favorite fishing pier. And, you must understand, I am an aficionado of piers. I've fished some classic piers along the east coast, both concrete and wooden. In some ways, the old worn wooden ones are the best spots on the planet to fish. I feel the same way about them as I do old wooden roller coasters and traditional bows: that's how they were meant to be. Granted, I enjoy the high-tech piers with concrete walkways, steel grating, steel rails, steel benches, and steel light posts. But the thrill of them, like new roller coasters, seems to wear out too fast. You can't take your knife and cut a notch in which to rest your rod tip in a steel rail. I am too nostalgic for splintering wood stained by years of salt water and wind. In January 1996, the *Sportfishing Report* published an article of mine entitled "Pier Pressure" in which I waxed nostalgic about fishing on the piers of North Carolina when I was a kid:

> There's something about fishing from a pier— particularly an Outer Banks pier—that makes me nostalgic for the simplicities of fishing. Don't get me wrong, I certainly relish fishing from a bridge, or a boat, or a beach, but a pier is something else. The nicked wooden rails speckled with scales, dried bait rotting between the planks, tourists tripping over your tackle boxes, drunk old men proffering useless wisdom, rusted and snagged hooks dangling from the rails; I guess when it comes down to it, I'm just a nostalgic romantic at heart.

Yet, despite my love for the classic piers, I am soulbound to the concrete and steel of Sebastian as well. I can't for certain say that I've fished this pier more than any other, but I'd take the bet I have. I have also had one of the most romantic moments of my life on this pier, a moment I keep tucked away in the private back rooms of my memory to be recalled when needed most. I assure you, however, that this moment did indeed involve one of the most beautiful women I've ever known, not a redfish. I also have had moments with redfish on Sebastian pier, and though thrilling, none were even remotely romantic.

Fishing for the really big redfish from Sebastian is relatively simple though often frustrating, as one can expect to lose much tackle to the rocks, cables, broken fishing line, and vegetation that tangles the bottom of Sebastian Inlet. The water is rarely still in the inlet, pouring in and out with powerful tides. On outgoing tides in the winter months, lures cast directly south into the inlet are swept east so fast that reeling in nothing but two-ounce spoons becomes a battle. In these winter months, big redfish hover at the outside of the mouth of the inlet, waiting to grab bait fish as they leave with the tide. I have come to learn, through conversation and the loss of countless spoons, that beyond the end of the jetty at the end of the pier there is a rise of rock and cable behind which the reds wait in ambush. Reaching this rise with casting gear is difficult, so those in the know bring 11- to 15-foot surf casting rods to the south-east corner of the pier. In the winter, the pier is usually stacked shoulder to shoulder with anglers, so room to work is scarce and tangles are common.

Using the long surf casting outfits, two to three ounce gold Gator or Krocodile spoons are cast as far out as possible. When the lure crashes into the fast-moving water, bails are left open to free spool the line out. The outgoing tide carries the spoon over the rise, and just as the bail is closed and the lure action increases with the taut line, big reds will grab the spoons and use the current coupled with their shoulders to fight. Of course, the tide and the spoons don't always work together, and the lures often sink into the rocks before crossing the rise. I always expect to lose 10 to 15 big spoons each day (at $3 to $5 a spoon, this is no cheap endeavor), though many lose more and some less. This far out on the pier, the water below is broken by a jetty, so even in close, lures snag and break off easily. But the reds that do hit are worth every lost spoon, every ounce of energy it takes to force them back into the high-speed water.

A few years back, I locked into six or seven of these monster reds in one day and lost all but one. I was using an 11-foot, heavy action spinning outfit rigged with 30-pound monofilament tied to a tapering of leaders to 100 pounds. When I finally pulled the one fish in close enough for anglers observing the battle to drop a dip net with an extended handle (nets are extremely necessary at Sebastian) and bring my fish to deck, I was so thrilled that I asked an onlooker to snap a few pictures for me with the small camera I keep in my tackle bag. Usually I wouldn't have asked someone to snap the pictures, because I don't like to encourage tourists to bother me, but I wanted to have proof of this fish. I estimated then, and will stick by that estimation, that the fish pushed the 50-pound mark. Granted, reds have been known to reach 90 pounds, but this was certainly the largest I had ever landed. Unfortunately, as I was releasing the red back to the water, some jackass grabbed my camera from where I had laid it in my open tackle bag. I'm not sure what other pictures were on that roll of film, but losing those photos of the red still ticks me off. Of course, now that red exists only in the realm of fish stories, and without that photo, everyone will assume that the red has grown a little since the last time I told the tale.

I've given up a lot on piers these days simply because of that camera and a few other incidents which have led me to believe that fishing where other humans are is just a pain in the ass. Roy and I used to night fish at the Skyway pier in St. Petersburg, and we used to watch drunk rednecks slaughter countless sailcats and rays and skates simply because "we don't wanna catch em again." It's a damn shame that piers are beginning to show the same signs of decline in the clientele that the rest of the world sees every day. Piers used to be a place to go to grow up, to learn about fishing, to learn from old men about the important stuff. Now they're mostly loaded with tourists and assholes, and rarely are they quiet.

Before I go on about redfish, about which this chapter claims to be, I do want to recount one other thing about Sebastian pier, something that has bothered me for a long time. Many summers ago, I don't recall exactly when, I was fishing the north side of the pier, casting a gold Rat-L-Trap, or occasionally a pencil jig, to small Spanish mackerel. The water was a spectacular clear green, and I could see a dark patch on the bottom of a hundred or so large snook lurking among the rocks. Occasionally a manatee would come to the surface, and the birds were thick about the pier as many fish were being taken. I would have been lost in the experience of this near-perfect Florida summer day if it hadn't been for the sheer numbers of people that were crammed shoulder to shoulder on the pier. I watched as several pelicans and seagulls grabbed baits and were dragged squawking to the pier where one grey-haired woman in a straw hat tied to her head with a light blue scarf would curse, put down her rod, and help whatever tourist was trying to dislodge hooks from feathers and beaks while berating the angler for his or her incompetence. She was getting angrier and angrier at the people mishandling the birds, and I didn't blame her. I half expected the tourists to start killing the birds and to once again hear "we don't wanna catch em again." As I cast again and again, my attention kept leaping to whatever activity happened to be the loudest at the moment. Not the sort of distractions I look for when fishing.

In my distraction, I paid little attention to my casting. With one whip of my rod, however, I felt the tip smack sharply into something solid, and immediately a small white gull tumbled from the sky and landed between a young man wearing a University of Wisconsin T-shirt and the bird-rescuing woman. Before the poor guy next to me knew what had happened, the woman had scooped up the wounded bird and began shouting at the guy: "You sonofabitch! Look what you did! You broke its neck! Now you gotta kill it!" She thrust the dying bird toward the guy's face demanding he kill the suffering animal. The poor kid was so stunned, so afraid, he couldn't even get out the words, "I didn't do it." It wouldn't have mattered if he had been able to; the woman would have had none of it. In her rage and yelling about the guy's stupidity, she grabbed the gull by the neck, twisted, and flung the dead bird to the water.

I was terrified. I was nauseous from realizing what I had done, and sure didn't want to face the wrath of the old bird woman. So, I cowardly grabbed my tackle bag and rod and left. She was still cursing the Wisconsin guy when I walked away. To this day I feel guilty about that incident, about killing the bird, about not accepting the responsibility, about leaving that poor guy to take the heat. It's one of those things that goes on my top ten list of things I should have done differently, things, that if given the chance to do again, I would do differently. It's the one dark spot I have about Sebastian, and perhaps one of the reasons I go back so often.

I suppose that one of the things I like about fishing for redfish is that reds tend to cruise in some of the places I like most: Sebastian, the shoal waters of North Carolina's Outer Banks, and just about any body of salienated water in Florida. I love salt water in Florida. Reds are a diverse bunch of fish, but boy have they got the right idea about where to live. Some days they may be holed up off the rise at Sebastian Inlet and on others they may be cruising lazily in the skinny waters of the Gulf of Mexico. Most likely they're in both places, but playing that elusive game of hide and seek at which they are experts. Occasionally, however, they give signs as to where they are: tailing on the flats, crashing schools of baitfish, humping the water as birds fly overhead, or just cruising in schools so thick they push the water out of their way. There is something tremendously powerful about watching the V-shaped wake of a school of reds cruising in shallow flats. Their strong shoulders push the water in front of them like a submarine moving through blue water. I must confess, also, that I have probably learned more about catching redfish by not catching them, by being frustrated at knowing they were there but not being able to hook them. I have certainly learned a lot about reds and catching reds from what many have written, but the frustration of trial and error is a much better teacher than most writers (sorry, Vic).

I have seen the phenomenon of schooling, feeding reds many times and chased these fish often. It's rare to be able to get close enough to cast to them when they're moving like this. I distinctly recall one summer fishing with Roy and Rob on the flats of Tampa Bay near MacDill Air Force Base when a school of nearly a hundred big reds began pushing water and scattering bait. For hours we would run up on them, cut the engine of the small jon boat, and cast, only to see the fish now hundreds of yards away. For nearly a full day we chased these reds, poling, paddling, rowing, motoring, and cursing, every approach we could think to use. Roy finally became so frustrated he leapt from the boat while under power and waded after them through the thick summer bay grasses. He managed to hook a keeper with a pink jig tail on a red lead head. I was so jealous of that fish. But Roy was forced to listen to my stories of bigger and more numerous reds as he and Stormy moved to Dallas that same summer.

Perhaps the most exciting redfishing I have ever done is that which I did on my home water river. As I have said before, this is perhaps the place I love fishing most, and place is so important. Often at night, here in Kansas, I have a recurring dream, one that I had as a teenager that peeks out of the back rooms of my mind from time to time. In this dream, I stand on the poling platform of a flats boat or a jon boat. The engine is off, and I wear only shorts. Sun pleasant and warm; water flat, clear, green. There is a light breeze pushing the boat across the southern flats. And from this perspective, the boat does not float across the water; rather, the world rolls by under my hull. I am the stable point, and the world slides by beneath me. I know this is an egotistical position in which I dream myself, but it is a sensation that I know when awake. I can stand on the highest point of a boat—the poling platform, the casting deck, the fly bridge—and somehow the world starts to slide beneath the hull. On my home waters, I often set a drift pattern across the Gulf flats that can take me hours before I have to readjust the boat. From here I cast and let the world slide by beneath.

For most of the year I blind cast from this position; sometimes I can sight cast to reds or cobia or tarpon. But casting gold spoons or topwaters or plastics or saltwater flies without knowing what's there is a thrill. And when a redfish does me the honor of grabbing my hook, those are the best redfish to catch, the ones that interrupt the drift, that stop the world from drifting by, that send my attention plummeting into the water like the white sprayed crash of a pelican. Those are the redfish that remind me that the world isn't drifting by, that it can crash in around me at any moment. Those are the heart-pounding excitements that have addicted me to angling. While there are days I wish I could float above the world with the ospreys and simply snag my fish from the water, most days I want to feel the spray of the water, the power of the red, the strain of the battle.

Yet, the redfish doesn't do this for me by some divine inspiration; it is not there for my own pleasure. The redfish splashes, fights, runs, bleeds, strains because it wants to survive. There may be, as I have said, a need for a masterwork exuding their beauty, but there is no redfish beauty beyond the aesthetic we attribute to it. The redfish needs first, foremost, and last to survive. Their beauty is in our eyes.

Discussing their prowess as representative of some facet or extension of human existence would be pointless if not shameful. We have done to redfish populations what we have done to so many others on this planet: literally chewed them until their numbers dwindled. We have eaten our way through this planet to the point of depleting a majority of our food supplies and depleting stocks of prey foods to the point where not only are those populations in danger of extinction, but we ourselves face the threat of having few prey species on which to feed. The redfish stands as a prime (rib) example, and those who know redfish are critically aware of what has happened to their numbers. Authors of instructional fishing books such as Robert J. Goldstein, author of *Coastal Fishing in the Carolinas: From Surf, Pier and Jetty*, have but only to turn to discussing redfish and how to catch them to be compelled to include citations explaining that "commercial fishermen take numbers of them in nets fixed near river deltas." And in *The Illustrated Encyclopedia of Fly-Fishing*, Silvo Calabi's listing for redfish points the finger at the cause of the demand for redfish flesh: "In the early 1980s redfish were severely over harvested in the Gulf of Mexico; the demand was apparently spurred by Cajun chef Paul Prudhomme's trendy blackened redfish entree."

Now, I do want to give credit here too. Humans recognized the plight of the redfish and reacted in ways that have allowed their populations to rejuvenate. Calabi is right to follow his critique of overfishing by acknowledging that "Strict regulations and controlled fishing brought the species back within a few years." While I wouldn't agree that the species is "back," legislation in Florida and other coastal states that limits the means by which fish are harvested and the numbers of fish that may be taken have provided the opportunity for populations to rebuild. And while I'm glad to see this, I have to wonder what all the joy is about. We have begun to pat ourselves on the back for recognizing that we have the ability to single out particular species of animals and decide whether or not they should be harvested until extinction or allowed to flourish. That's a damn pompous power for us to have. We cannot float above this world and take what we choose as though the planet were one grand buffet.

But, I do want to confess here that I'm torn about harvesting fish; after all, I wouldn't have undertaken the endeavor of writing this book if I didn't hold a deep love for doing so myself. I face a similar conflict as did the great Florida Naturalist Archie Carr, who explained that he was always torn between his desire to study Florida wildlife and wanting to eat most of it. For the most part, I practice a catch and release ethic, though I do keep an occasional red (or other fish) for the dinner table. The truth of it is, I would keep a fish a day and eat nothing but, if the opportunity were afforded me to fish each day (and if I were blessed with the ability not to be skunked regularly). I would do so not only because I love the flesh of a fish, but because doing so is important; it is important to know from where our food comes. It is important to take responsibility (even if only once in a while) for the food we put in our bellies. I would be as much a subsistence fisherman as possible, but the world has taken that away from us. Doing so would mean giving up work, and bills must be paid. Doing so would mean finding plentiful supplies of fish, but the world has reduced fish populations to the point that reliable catching just doesn't happen. So I am careful to release, to keep only once in a while, when that craving for good meat to go with my grits gets too strong.

And let's face it, the fish I could get at the supermarket is just crap. I recently wanted to make a pot of Chokoloskee Chowder (my recipe a bastardized version of Totch Brown's recipe in *Totch*) for a party I was having here in Kansas. I missed the spicy fish soup in my homesickness and thought to recreate a version on my Kansas stove. At the store, pale grey slabs lay in the glass display case labeled "Special! Marlin steaks!" Outraged, I called the manager over and demanded he stop purchasing billfish, and then asked how long the meat had been on display. He wasn't sure. When I asked about the oysters (still in their shells) he said they'd been there for "two or three weeks, but they've been on ice." And so my chowder was made from canned shrimp, canned crab, and "farm-raised catfish nuggets." After all, I had promised chowder to a bunch of Midwesterners; how the hell would they know. My culinary homesickness was not cured.

I've had to accept the resolve that fresh fish is just not to be a part of my life here. I have heard, however, from Roy, down in Dallas now, that there is a lake used to cool a power plant somewhere in Texas which holds stocked reds. Apparently, the power plant keeps the water warm enough for the reds, which have the ability to move from salt to fresh water, to survive, though these fish never see salt water. Though I'm a little wary about the actual sport involved in catching reds that are dumped and then trapped in a small contained lake, I may just have to give in and drive the truck down there and toss a few gold spoons their way. My guess is that a power plant outflow would probably be my least favorite place to catch reds. I imagine the experience to be like trying to eat a ball park hot dog somewhere other than in a ball park—the thing's edible, but it's just not the same. The place where an event happens often make the event worth experiencing. Like I said, place is so important.

So, maybe instead of driving to Texas, maybe I'll just sit here in redfish-free Kansas and dream of other places, of big redfish. I can take a medium action spinning outfit down out of the racks, tie on a plug that today looks to me to be the exact thing a big, Mack-truck-sized red would want to grab. I can sit and imagine myself standing there on the casting deck of a boat which is free drifting across grass flats and oyster bars in the warm fall sun of a Florida west coast autumn. I can feel the flex and snap of the rod, hear the soft whir of the line speeding out past the bail to the first guide. Watching, I see the plug torpedo through the air in a perfect arc across a blue-sky background, plopping with the faintest splash into the golden-green water 50 yards ahead of me. Begin the retrieve. Slow, because redfish don't want to chase fast moving food; it's too damn hot even now in the autumn waters to be anything but sluggish in the search for food. Slow retrieve; twitch the rod tip; work the lure; walk the dog. And there, behind the shallow running plug, a distinct V wake pushing up behind the artificial. A sudden rush of panic; don't stop reeling in the excitement. Slow, a twitch here and there, and suddenly, with a rush of power, a big boil and the lure stops coming in freely. Heart suddenly beating faster; rod lifted solid in setting the hook. And the fight.

A thousand miles away, that's how I would spend the day. But to be honest about it, today I'd be happy even if the fish didn't come, if I had the chance to simply float across Gulf flats and feel the sun. To feel those other things that draw me to fishing. To listen to the rap of the water on the hull. To watch the glide of a white pelican. To hear the wet exhale of porpoises. To catch a glimpse of a loggerhead. To see a ray fly past below my bow. To feel the scream of an osprey in my ears. To taste the Gulf on my tongue. Today I would want to be alone in the church of salt water no matter if the reds should appease me by boiling my baits or not.

For me, that is what makes being in the place of redfish so important. In those places where redfish and I run, I can see the things that make the world beautiful. I often find myself, while on fishing expeditions, laying aside the tackle and just watching: the flow of the tide, the ripples of wind on the water, the motion of the things that swim, the grace of the things that fly.

I know it's probably cliched to say so, but I think a lot of us have forgotten how to see things, to watch things. Recently I spent some time with my parents at the cottage in Kitty

Hawk. One day I was carefully watching three or four schools of menhaden that were slowly making their way north about 200 yards off the beach. I pointed them out to my father, and together we watched for game fish to smash the schools. We caught glimpses of Spanish mackerel torpedoing out of the water here and there, but never in the thick of the menhaden. As we watched, my mother asked me to teach her how to see those things. For the next two days we talked about the different ripples menhaden make on the water, how to distinguish them from wind brushing the water, how to tell menhaden from other bait, and how to watch osprey and gulls and pelicans to tell where fish were. At the end of those two days, on a breezy day when the water was choppy and speckled with greybeards, I asked her to point out the two menhaden schools, to read their signature in a chaos of movement. She found them both and asked me how I learned to see those things. I reminded her that she had taught me a lot about watching and reading the world. We talked about watching, about paying attention, about learning to read nature just as we would learn to read any other language. Today, I would like to read those pages where the redfish run.

Blues

If redfish have stolen my passion, then bluefish have been my obsession. There is no question that for every fish I've dreamed of catching, I've actually caught twice as many in numbers of bluefish. During the days of my first rod on Outer Banks' beaches, I kept index card records of the hundreds of tailor blues I would haul in. I've spent cold February and November days standing on North Carolina beaches with my father and mother, with friends, or alone waiting for the feeding-frenzy blitzes for which the Outer Banks are famous. I've stood on the Oregon Inlet Bridge straining against heavy pier tackle trying to keep big blues from running into the tangles of line of dozens of anglers standing shoulder to shoulder fighting slashing autumn blues.

And I've stood on the very pier at Sebastian where the giant reds became part of my life and hauled in three to five-pound blues in December until my shoulders ached and cramped under the tension of bluefish battles. From half-pound juveniles to ferocious 20-pound-class monsters, bluefish and I have fought more times than I could ever count.

There's no real trick to catching blues; any slob of a fisherman can do it. When they're hitting, they hit anything. And I mean anything. I've taken blues on bucktails, plastics, pencil jigs, cut bait, live bait, topwaters, spoons, poppers, bottom rigs, divers, empty hooks, and yes, even hooks baited with carrot pieces or strips of rags. I've caught them running deep, trolling, jigging, drifting, kite fishing, and on clothespin rigs. I've caught them when I've been looking for them, and I've caught them when I was fishing for other species. I've sight casted to them in the calm green seas of a late summer Gulf of Mexico, and I've hurled huge metal spoons with a fifteen foot rod into the angry churning grey waters of a late winter Cape Hatteras. The methods may vary, but the strategy remains the same: if there are bluefish there, they'll eat anything in their path. It makes the angling strategy rather simple, and it makes showing off to visiting anglers rather easy.

When I first started writing about fishing some years ago, it seemed only natural that I write about bluefish. After all, if there's one sort of fishing to which I can claim expertise, it would have to be bluefishing. At the time I started writing about bluefishing, however, I wasn't looking to share my expertise or even make claims to expertise. I wrote out of guilt. I've mentioned my (thankfully) brief venture into poetry; I won't torture you with another of my verses. However, I will mention this one particular poem in which I tried to come to terms with the fact that not only have I caught lots of bluefish, but I have also killed lots of them. In this particular poem I spent entirely too many verses expounding upon how the seas became angry with me for unnecessarily killing dozens of bluefish that never saw way to my table. I'm not sure if I realized then the importance of my revelation, but at the time I was becoming a catch-and-release fisherman, and the guilt of dead blues was pushing me there.

But let me also be clear that while I did senselessly kill a lot of those bluefish many years ago, most of the fish I killed I ate. I was not, as I might have suggested, simply killing bluefish to be able to stack their corpses like cord wood; I was chewing their meat. Now, many a connoisseur of fish flesh will tell you that blues just aren't worth eating, that the meat is too bloody and too fishy. I disagree wholeheartedly. If a bluefish is bled out immediately, then the meat is firm and tasty, and butter-fried bluefish is delicious. Bleeding out the fish is simple: just slice its throat as soon as it is landed and put the fish in salt water. The water will draw the blood out. When cleaning the fish, rather than skinning it out, I prefer to take the time to scale it and leave the skin on (a wonderful thing to nibble after it's been fried crisp in butter), and the dark blood line which runs laterally through the fish along the backbone should be removed. I assure you that I am such a fan of this fare that when I was in kindergarten and was asked what my favorite food was, my response was butter-fried bluefish. In fact, when the teacher asked us to write directions about how to make our favorite food so that she might compile them into a kindergarten cookbook to give to our parents, my recipe was rather simple: "Catch bluefish. Clean Bluefish. Fry in Butter. Eat." Notice that even at the ripe young age of five my recipe begins with "catch bluefish" rather than "go to store" as did most of my classmates' recipes. Had the excitement of my first publication not clouded my thinking, I probably would have suggested churning your own butter too.

Unlike the redfish, whose beauty, strength, and prowess as a sportfish have not been extolled in a book-length tribute, the bluefish has earned a text of celebration. I speak, of course, of

John Hersey's *Blues.* In this wonderful book, Hersey mirror's Izaak Walton's conversation between *Piscator* and *Venator* with his own Fisherman and Stranger conversation. Unlike any other treatment of the habits and lives of bluefish, Hersey weaves together a wealth of information about blues in a great read. No other text conveys such descriptive prose about bluefish. One of my favorite passages regarding the ferocity with which these fish eat and live comes early in the lesson when the Fisherman first takes the Stranger fishing for blues and the Stranger asks, "Will I really know when one is on?" The Fisherman responds to his student:

> *Will you ever! Blues strike like blacksmiths' hammers. In fact, what will occur to you first about these animals is that they are vicious; it will take time for you to see what truly beautiful mechanisms they are. Back in 1871, Professor Spenser Fullerton Baird, who became the first head of the now defunct U.S. Commission of Fish and Fisheries, rightly called the bluefish "an animated chopping machine." He described how a school of blues rove like a pack of hungry wolves, destroying everything in sight, leaving a trail of fragments from their prey and a stain of blood and oil on the sea. Some fish masticate their food; blues chop and swallow big hunks. In 1965, commercial fishermen, out at sea in pursuit of a fish called menhaden, which is used in the manufacture of fertilizer, told of having plowed through a thirty-mile-wide school of blues macerating hordes of menhaden. Feeding along coasts, blues have driven terrified menhaden up on beaches until they were piled a foot deep. Professor Baird estimated that in four summer months off the New England Coast blues killed twelve hundred million fish. That estimate may have been high, but there is no question that blues are both*

butchers and gluttons. They're cannibals that will eat their young. They will eat anything alive. They have stripped the toes from surfers in Florida. They make the excesses of Huron feasts—at one of which, in 1635, a host served his guests twenty deer and four bears—seem, by comparison, genteel repasts. It's a myth, though, that blues will eat till full, like Romans, then vomit and eat again; that would be maladaptive. But they can't not eat; they can't suppress the urge to kill. If you paint sheep with lithium chloride, their predators soon learn it makes them sick, and they will no longer attack the sheep. But paint rabbits with poison and the hawk can't help itself, it will swoop and kill, even when sick from having eaten poisoned rabbits. The blue has the same dedication. "It is a hard thing to persuade the belly, because it hath no ears."

I've seen blues do these very things. I've seen them herd menhaden in the surf until the small fish beach themselves in a suicidal fear. I'd like to think that the menhaden are noble and chose to face death by their own volition rather than at the slashing teeth of the blues—an ichtheological Masada. And, I have seen those very bluefish beach themselves while chasing the menhaden. There is something wondrous about an animal which will kill itself in the pursuit of food. I've also seen surfers paddle in panic as a school of blues move into an area, and I have seen teeth marks in their surfboards.

But, despite the veracity with which they devour their way through life—or perhaps because of it—blues are beautiful animals. They are alert when taken to boat, eyes intelligent and cunning, their bodies streamlined and solid with muscle. They seem at all times healthy and determined in their ways. I once watched from on high a school of thirty or so large blues cruise through a drop-off trough just off of the beach.

They moved with the resolution of the unconquerable. When they crossed paths with a school of small baitfish, they slashed and cut until the bait pod was no more than an oil slick of fish pieces. Even the small sand shark that came to investigate the activity turned tail when it recognized the source of the mayhem. The blues returned to their course as though the small baitfish massacre had never happened. These fish had grit.

I admire the veracity and single-mindedness with which blues proceed through life. Whenever playing that ridiculous cocktail party game wherein people try to figure out to what animal they are kindred spirits, I often wish I could claim kinship with the bluefish, but the blue has no mercy and I get distracted too easily. I'd be slaughtered by my own school if I tried to make my living as a blue. Though, to admit it, my species of animal is actually much more adept at mass slaughter; at least blues do so for a purpose.

Perhaps that's one of the reasons I enjoy battling blues so much. There's something primal about tugging on a line that is hooked to a pissed-off package of killing meat. I like the sensation of feeling the other end pull back, of the strength that an organism whose single agenda is survival can produce when threatened. And to confess, I like when the blue beats me, when the line breaks, the hooks pulls free, the line runs out, the rod breaks. I like the frustration of having been beaten by that mechanism. I laugh then. I am of the firm belief that the fish that beat us are the more fun fish with which to tangle. "Learn to set the hook!" Roy will chide me. But my slow reaction, my bad technique, my overeagerness to horse the fish, that's when the fish wins, when it finds an angler's weakness, an angler's fault, and it exploits that moment for its own survival. The rush of frustration when something we so often think of as a stupid fish has beaten us at our own game is exquisite. To those fish I mimic old Papa Hemingway and say "Thank you, fish." Those are the fish to count as trophies, the ones smarter and stronger than we. When instinct beats rationality.

Yes, bluefish have become a large part of my life. Sitting here now, so far from even the smallest of tailor blue, so far from a blitz, I realize that I have honored the bluefish in my home with pictures and iconery. Hanging above my front door, welcoming all who come to my home, hangs a wooden bluefish I cut, carved, sanded, stained, and polyurethaned from an old plank I found floating in salt water somewhere. It is distinctly a blue: torpedo body, thick tail, firm-set jaw. I honed it from wood to stand guard at my door, to identify to those who come knocking that a catcher of blues resides within. I think I would have liked it if George Bush had hung a carved bluefish over the door at the White House when he lived there. He was, after all, a catcher of blues, and as Howell Raines notes in *Fly Fishing Through the Midlife Crisis*, he is a supporter of light-tackle fishing for blues. In fact, all presidents who are anglers should hang carved fish on the door to let us know where they stand. Raines has a chapter in his book about fishing presidents which is intriguing. His credentials gave him the opportunity to meet presidents and to talk fishing with them. Lucky bastard. If you're going to talk fishing with someone, world leaders seem like a fun bunch with whom to shoot the shit. I can hear the hunting conversations too: "Yup. I just got me a new 12 gauge. What you using this season, George?" "ICBM." "Yup."

Personally, I love the stories Jimmy Carter tells in *An Outdoor Journal* about arranging diplomatic tours around fishing or about sneaking out of the White House to cast a few. That's a man who has his priorities down. I wrote Carter on the occasion of his birthday one year to compliment him on *An Outdoor Journal* and the fishing stories told therein. I never expected to hear from him, figuring to get a boilerplate thank you note from a staff member, but sure enough he wrote back to thank me for my letter. His reply was short, but heartfelt. It meant a lot to me. I showed it to everyone I knew. So, last month when Carter was in Kansas City signing copies of his just released *Living Faith*, I decided to take the opportunity to introduce myself. If Raines could talk fishing with presidents, then so could I. What I didn't realize was that when a former president turns out to sign books, about ten thousand other people also want to meet him. When I arrived at the signing location, I found out I was number 1,598 to get my books signed. The 1,597 other people had arrived earlier, and another 8,000 or so would arrive after I did.

To give a good picture of how the signing goes, one of Carter's assistants told me that he signs close to 2,000 books in a session. He doesn't talk to well-wishers. He sits at a table, head down, pen rolling. Lines of visitors are herded cattle style through corrals much like the lines at Disney—a company that has mastered human herding. Books are handed, opened to the page which one wants signed, to an assistant who passes it to another assistant who passes it under Carter's perpetually moving pen. If a person wants a photo, the camera is handed to an assistant who watches for the person to pass in front of the former president. The staffer hollers "Photo!" and Carter lifts his head, pen never stopping, smiles, and returns to his signing. No recognition of the person who will later hang the picture along with other family photos.

Well, I decided that I wasn't going to miss an opportunity, so when my moment of passing the former president came, I stopped, called out, "Mr. President, it's me, Sid Dobrin. You wrote to me." And as I did, I stopped walking; eight thousand other people also stopped walking. The books stopped passing. Carter stopped signing. He looked up, curious as to why the whole process had stopped. I repeated my name, certain that he'd heard me. Befuddled by the breakdown, he looked at me and said, "Yes? Oh, hi." At this point men in dark suits were whispering into their lapels all around the room; assistants were panicking. Things were not supposed to stop. Stopping is apparently a bad thing. The former president was not supposed to be talking to strangers. Strangers are apparently bad things. Sensing that the 8,000 people behind me and the Secret Service and all of the assistants were not going to let my private conversation go on much longer, I leaned across the corral rope to the table and asked the President, "Any chance I could get some time to talk with you when you are finished here?" Carter stared at me blankly. The Secret Service agents were moving straight for me, and Carter was obviously caught off guard. "I—I don't know," he replied, "check with my assistant." With that last syllable, two hands grabbed me by the arms, led me toward the door, and I saw Carter hunch back over and his pen start signing again. Eight thousand people got back to their mooing and marching.

I never did get to talk with the former president. The Secret Service escorted me out into the snow, and the one assistant who would hear my pleas informed me that the President was entirely too busy on this tour to readjust his current schedule. If I wanted to set up a meeting, I could contact the Carter Foundation for further assistance.

I think we would have gotten along. I know I could jaw on and on about fishing with the guys who run the world; after all, they're just guys. I sent Carter a second letter inviting him to write a foreword to this book. This time, I did get a form letter from an assistant informing me that the former president was entirely too busy to accept my invitation. Oh well, I think Flip Pallot has done a dandy job, and he's never been too busy to talk to me. Flip would make a good president, and I bet he'd hang a wooden fish on the door.

I like it when presidents are fishermen. There's something deeply American about it. Bush, Carter, Hoover, Cleveland. One has to figure that no matter what other faults that individual has as person or politician, at least there's one redeeming quality in him. There have been some nonfishing presidents who are questionable to the core. At least the ones who fish have had some of the experiences that make people better people. At least their daddies taught them a thing or two about living. I just question their desire to take a job that doesn't leave one much time for doing the important things like fishing, for being able to go to the places where fishing happens. The places where fishing happens are important places.

There's a huge shifting sand dune on the Outer Banks of North Carolina named Jockey's Ridge. At least once a year I make my way to the top of Jockey's Ridge and look out across the beautiful expanse of the Outer Banks. For more than 20 years I've been making this minor pilgrimage to survey the changing layout of the beaches, roads, and buildings. This used to be more of a spiritual excursion for me, but recently, I have to admit, I've begun to lose sight of the spirituality. The scattering of cottages that once artistically dotted the beaches and dunes have been replaced with rows of condos, shopping centers, traffic jams, and overmanicured lawns.

Okay, let me rant here: lawns on a beach? I once watched a couple lay sod at their new waterfront home in Seward, Alaska. I wanted so badly to point out to them that the roots of their precious grass would not tolerate the salt water which came crashing into their backyard every day, but I held my tongue. I reveled the next year when I noticed that the hundreds of dollars worth of sod had been replaced by gravel and sand. I don't think we'll ever figure out that we simply can't manicure nature to our liking all of the time. To reconcile, it has often seemed to me that what the Outer Banks needs most is a good dose of napalm and about a million or so years to return it to what it used to be. I know that saying such things is heresy these days—after all, the Outer Banks residents have certainly prospered from tourist money and growth. But I tend to be curmudgeonly about a lot of things, and looking out across Kill Devil Hills these days, I can't help but long for those "old days."

In the parts of Virginia and North Carolina where I did a lot of my growing up, old timers often refer to themselves as "been heres," which stands in direct opposition to the "come heres" who don't have the history or family ties of a been here. Unfortunately, much as I would like, I can't claim to be a been here on the Outer Banks, though I often pretend. I'll always be a come here to most of the locals, and I do recognize the minor hypocrisy of thinking of the Outer Banks as part of my home. But, indulge me. I "come here" a lot, and the Outer Banks are a special part of my life. So, I long for the old days; what's wrong with that? To those of us who have known the Outer Banks for long periods of time, those days are easily defined: when the old mini-golf course still sat at the foot of Jockey's Ridge, before National Geographic listed it as one of the best mini-golf courses in the world, and before the shifting sands of Jockey's Ridge swallowed its big green octopus and castle. The days when the biggest grocery store around was the IGA in Manteo, and the Fisherman's Wharf in Wanchese really was a fisherman's wharf. There were days when one could still stand on the Oregon Inlet Bridge and pull huge bluefish from the churning water as they ran under the bridge in near endless schools. Those days when the beach road was *the* road, and the four lane bypass hadn't been built or seemed too far away to bother with once it was put in. Days when you could catch huge crabs right under a wooden statue of ol' Sir Walter Raleigh without coming across a single yacht, let alone massive commercial marinas. Days when the Coquina Beach parking lot was the biggest patch of pavement for miles (at least they've gotten rid of most of that now).

But as sure as I give my mind over to the notion that it's inevitable that one day someone will probably just pave over the entire beach so the tourists won't get sandy and that they'll serve tofu burgers at Sam and Omie's and that John's inshore or offshore fish sandwiches will be replaced by

McSimulated fish product, something always reminds me that this place does still retain enough of its spirit that we could never pave over it. Recently, in a visit to these waters, in an escape from the plainness of the Great Plains (I'm still not so sure what's so great about them), I was reminded of this more vividly than I'd ever remembered. Early in the summer, when the water was still cold enough that wearing waders was necessary, but late enough that the speckled trout had started hitting just after the sun peaked across the horizon and covered the beaches in fiery lights of pink, I found myself so lost in the spirit of Outer Banks fishing that they could have paved right over me and I'd never have noticed.

I was standing in the surf a hundred yards south of a fishing pier casting a tandem white bucktail rig with a light spinning outfit—I'll leave out which pier, since I'd still like to keep my favorite spots to myself, but if you know trout fishing from the beaches, you probably know this spot well, and you've probably seen me there many times. It was, of course, one of those perfect Outer Banks' mornings: shore-break waves, glassy water, osprey floating above, and that perfect sunrise. Things had been slow for the two previous days and only one or two other anglers were casting nearby, though a few more watched from the beach and the pier, sipping hot coffee from styrofoam cups, waiting to see if anything was biting before they'd even bother coming down to the sand. I've never understood the type of fishing wherein you drink coffee until someone else catches the fish; the logic of it baffles me. But, I too, wasn't convinced much of anything would happen, so I wasn't exactly paying that much attention to my casting.

Instead, my wandering mind took me to that place where all fishermen go, where dreams and reality become blended together and the light of the sunrise melts through your eyes and turns all that you know into reflections on the water. This is a magical place, a serene place; it is the place all fishermen write about, talk about. It is the place we would all stay could we only find the way. My mind, not quite fully awake in the early hours, had drifted to that place and left my arms to casting the eight-pound outfit on their own, and the casts had become carefree and methodic. My right arm whipped the rod to send the bucktails outside the breakers on the down beats of my metronome casting: tick, cast, reel; tick, cast, reel.

My mind traveled around to that rhythm, not thinking of anything in particular: loves past and lost, fish caught and lost. And there, in that place of the fisherman, I found the peace of water, of the Outer Banks and sighed with the morning breeze. My casting followed its rhythm and kept tempo with the crash of the surf. As I traveled around in those dusty old rooms in the back of my mind that I occasionally visit when there's not much else I need or want to think about and as my right arm went about its casting, a different methodic rhythm brought me back, somewhat, to the beach. A resounding crash that thudded in the wind every few minutes began to draw my attention and my eyes to the water searching for the source. It took me only moments to realize that what I was hearing was the slap of a humpback whale's pectorals on the water. This whale was only a hundred yards or so off the end of the pier and slowly moving south. It was lifting its massive right pectoral fin from the water and bringing it down with a deep thudding splash. Time and time again: thhuuud. Thhuuud. As I sat and watched this magical scene of whale and sea and sunrise, my arms continued in their rhythm of tick, cast, reel.

And again, I was lost to the spirit of salt water; the silhouetted whale against an early summer sunrise, so close, so active, brought me to a concentration and focus that was as blinding as the sun. And as if on cue, just as my mind completely let go of my casting, and my arms took full control again, line began screaming from my reel and the tension of a big fish nearly tore the rod from my hands.

I never saw the fish. I know it must have been a big blue from the way it ran. It tore so much line from my reel so fast that I had to try to sprint down the beach in my bulky waders just to keep from being spooled. Of course, my eight-pound gear was no match for the fish, which broke the line and disappeared. I carefully placed that moment away to be remembered another day when I stand casting, dreaming of loves and fish gone by.

During my futile exercise in chasing down the fish, I lost track of the whale. It probably continued its venture south toward Florida, lost in the rhythm of its morning, not caring too much that I was staring frustrated at the surf, looking for my lost fish and scrambling to re-rig with the hope that he was only one of a larger school, or that the beach road would be bumper to bumper with tourist-packed cars by Sunday afternoon.

It's moments like that, with bluefish and whales and sun and salt water, when my mind can let go of all of those things that cloud daily living. It's mornings like that, when my eight-pound spinning gear pulls in a small tailor blue while my mind dreams, when I am most at peace. Those early morning tailor blues that are bled, scaled, filleted, and butter fried with a hint of onion, cooked gently on an electric skillet on the back deck of the cottage with the sun just coming up, those are the fish that make fishing all the worthwhile. And though I have claimed an affinity for those fish that beat me, that win freedom, I will also say "thank you, fish" to those that make breakfast that much better. Those breakfasts are often eaten alone, before my parents and brothers come sleepy-eyed onto the porch to watch porpoises jump in what's left of the sunrise. I enjoy pulling the hot flesh from the pan with my fingers, licking the butter from the hands which have just caught and cleaned the very fish on which I chew. It feels good to know where I fit with my breakfast.

The old words, "If you don't eat the world, the world eats you," come to mind on mornings like this. And how true with a bluefish. Certainly that animal would chomp meat from my thigh if given the chance. I suppose that I think of bluefish the same way some people think of crappie or snapper or spot or whatever fish you first *really* learned to catch. Bluefish take me back to simpler times, when I could run up and down the beach chasing schools of chopper blues and not have to worry about anything else. When I learned bluefish, phone bills, office politics, and taxes were all foreign concepts to me. Catching bluefish was all that mattered on days when blue-fishing was happening. Today, getting lost in sunrise expeditions up and down beaches in search of bluefish are in some-ways expeditions for a simpler time. When wandering around in those carefully stowed-away memories that seem to open up so much more easily on bluefish mornings, I find a lot of recollections of younger, carefree days.

Catching bluefish is a child's game. As I said, any slob of a fisherman can do it, so it makes for easy fishing for young anglers to learn the ways of fish and water. And for those of us who do it as adults, there is certainly strain of gear and muscle, there is challenge of the tug-of-war with blues, but there is also the easiness of it. Bluefishing allows us to be chil-dren again, not to have to worry about the detail of things. There's no worry of right tackle or bait. The blues don't care; they're not picky. As far as prey, for us they are easy. They let us be young; they let us fish without work, without thought. I am so often reminded of Robert Traver's words when blue-fishing, and though Traver was a trout bum and devout fly fisherman, his words always come echoing back to me when the chance to hunt blues comes up: "After all, aren't fisher-men merely permanently spellbound juveniles who have traded in Santa Claus for Izaak Walton?" I know I am. I had a friend who used to always say to me, "Sid, you are such a boy." She was right. I get excited about the same things that boys get excited about: water, trees, fishing, playing ball, ice cream, exploring. I love the sensation of finding something new, of seeing the world in new ways for the first time. I like the excitement the world offers a child.

But on days when there are no bluefish around, when work seems overbearing, when salt water seems far away, when being an adult must take precedent over being a boy, when I can't quite find my way to those backroom memories, those are the days I wonder what's worth doing and what's not. I wish I had the courage to walk away from the world of work and worries and spend the rest of my life finding everything new I could about salt water. Flip Pallot did that. I envy him so. And when you watch Flip on television or when you talk to him in person, you can see that boyish excitement come creeping out. When he sees an alligator or a tarpon or an osprey or whatever, there's an amazement with the world in his eyes. After all, there is no thrill, no excitement like the thrill of wonder and discovery. Joseph Cambell said something similar: "the inhabiting spirit of life is awe." He's right. I would love to feel that excitement everyday, to be a boy rambling and exploring. It's like Penny Baxter says in Marjorie Kinnan Rawling's *The Yearling*: "What would I do this fine spring day, was I a boy? . . . I'd go rambling." Maybe Flip wouldn't make such a good president; I'd hate to see him confined to an office. It'd kill his spirit. Besides, if we are just children who have traded in Santa for Walton, then I suppose we should heed our patron saint's words: "There is no life, my honest scholar, no life so happy and so pleasant as the life of a well-governed angler."

Drink

Much as writers who fish write about fishing, writers who drink often pontificate about alcohol. In fact, it's often been noted that some of the greatest writers have also had reputations as formidable drinkers as well: Oscar Wilde, John Steinbeck, F. Scott Fitzgerald, Edgar Allan Poe, Dylan Thomas, Dave Barry, and of course Ernest Hemingway. One of my favorite writers, who often poured a little alcohol into his words (or maybe a few words into his alcohol), was William Faulkner. In *Go Down, Moses* Faulkner writes:

> There was always a bottle present, so that it
> would seem to him that those fine fierce instants of
> heart and brain and courage and wildness and speed

were concentrated and distilled into that brown liquor which not women, not boys and children, but only hunters drank, drinking not of the blood they spilled but some condensation of the wild immortal spirit, drinking it moderately, humbly even, not with the pagan's base and baseless hope of acquiring thereby the virtues of cunning and strength and speed but in salute to them. Thus it seemed to him on this December morning not only natural but actually fitting that this should have begun with whiskey.

Boy can some people write.

When I first started graduate school I had to give an impromptu talk on a short work of Faulkner. I think it was "A Rose for Emily." I was so nervous that I kept referring to the piece as Hemingway's "A Rose for Emily." It's actually funny because anyone who has read my fiction has accused me of reading too much Hemingway since my sentence construction tends often to mimic his. I never noticed. There's no doubt that I like Hemingway. I also like Faulkner. Probably because I enjoy drinking. These words of Faulkner's that I begin with are some of my favorite when it comes to words about drinking. My friend Chris deSantis, an American Literature scholar, recently reminded me of them.

But to be honest about it, drinking, particularly drinking as it intersects with fishing, is a difficult subject to write about. Not because the subject is difficult, but because in a lot of ways it is like talking about religion—a dangerous subject about which to write to an unfamiliar audience, and some, like myself, are as devout and as opinionated (maybe even fanatical in our rituals and beliefs) about drinking and fishing as many are about religion. So, let me begin by clarifying a few points: first, I am a drinker. I enjoy the escapist pleasures of alcohol, and I do enjoy drinking in wild places. In fact, drinking sometimes makes a place all the more wild. But let me be specific: I am a drinker, not a drunk. I simply don't have the stamina to be the latter. As Albert Collins sings, "I don't care what the people are thinking. I ain't drunk, I'm just drinking."

Also, let me clarify: I consider myself an outdoor writer, not a nature writer. And let me be specific again: there is a difference. A nature writer is an artist who paints beautiful scenery with words and who takes readers by the hands and shows them beautiful places in the natural world. An outdoor writer tells the general public about beautiful places where the hunting, fishing, and camping are good, thus exposing the outdoor world to the masses, which in turn helps make those natural places into crowded, overused places about which nature writers would have no desire to write.

I differentiate between the two professions here purposefully, mostly because my recent thinking about the two insist upon division, but also because as I think about rhetoric, about writing, about language, about the academic things for which I get paid to think, I recognize that the differences are rhetorical and that what we do as writers of nature is that we expose those places when we write. And, I do mean this literally—that we *write* nature, we *write* the place. And by exposing those places, as I've said in earlier chapters, we make them vulnerable. The outdoor writer gets paid for doing so; kickbacks and payola are standard for outdoor writers. Outdoor writers tell readers where to go, how to gain access to places; nature writers are just more subtle about it. Even the most valiant attempts to keep a place secret—such as Barry Lopez's description of the stone horse, which I mentioned earlier— leave readers wanting to find a place, or at least a place much like the one about which they've read. Extreme examples range from the lake in *On Golden Pond* to the rivers of *A River Runs Through It*, both now crowded and popular.

But so as not to make this preamble seem a rant that has nothing to do with the crux of what I want to say here, let me say this: despite the differences I recognize between outdoor and nature writers, when it comes to writing about ways in which drinking intersects with our experiences in the wild, both are generally quite willing to hide the fact that drinking and nature do intersect. When I ask other writers why they don't write about drinking in the wild, I am frequently told, "This is a subject I try to avoid in my writing."

Well, I don't. As you may recognize by now, I consider myself a fisherman. I grew up in a family where fishing and salt water are dominant forces. My grandfather and his brother fished for a living. I worked at a marina for six years. I write for fishing magazines and teach fishing literature. And if I've learned anything about fishing over the years, it's that fishermen drink. Now I don't mean that all fishermen drink all of the time, but the culture of drinking is unquestionably a large part of the American fishing culture. In fact, in my travels, I've come across enough evidence supporting this assumption that I don't need to construct a stereotypical fishing trip for you in which more Budweiser is stuffed into the boat than is bait. In Tennessee, a billboard for Ice House Beer depicts a picture of a case of the product above which two words are painted: "Fishing Lure." I can't even begin to count the number of tackle shops I've visited whose signs proclaim "Beer, Bait, and Tackle" as though the priority is definitive. And the store next to the fishing lake in South Georgia which proclaims "coldest beer on the lake!" Or how about Ray Stevens' hit song which warns "Don't go fishin with a man who's been drinkin'." Yep, Ray Stevens is still making records.

So when outdoor writers tell me they avoid writing about drinking and fishing, I hear them say that they avoid writing about what many Americans see as an essential element to the activity of fishing. When I first moved to Kansas, many of my new friends and colleagues made every effort to prove to me that Kansas could be as wonderful a fishing environment as were my Florida and coastal Virginia and North Carolina homes; they introduced me to something called ice fishing.

Not being familiar with ice in any way other than in my drink, but devoutly attracted to any notion of fishing, I was curious. Then they told me that you don't go ice fishing for the fishing, you go for the brandy. And herein lies the contradiction to my complaint about outdoor writers and their honesty about fishing and drinking: I don't do it.

In America, fishing and drinking have become so enmeshed in centuries of tradition that contemporary tackle manufacturers have begun affixing plastic drink holders to nearly everything that remains within reach of the angler. Lorain Hemingway begins her essay "The Young Woman and the Sea" by explaining that "There was a cocktail party the night before. It was the second night of the third Annual Hemingway Billfishing Tournament, and many participants had been working on a decent, stabilizing drunk for several days. I had my share of beer. Enough to float one of the sunken sailboats in Bimini's harbor." How Hemingwayesque: alcohol and fishing. How much a part of the proud burden with which Lorain Hemingway struggles in carrying that name. How much a part of the culture of the angler that Ernest Hemingway portrayed and that anglers feel the compulsion to follow. And, when weekend hook-'n-wormers, open-ocean tournament fisherfolk, and all the other variety of anglers pack for a trip, one can assume they are carrying enough alcohol to help Lorain Hemingway refloat the entire flotilla at the bottom of Bimini Harbor.

I resist this tradition of drinking while fishing. I keep these two very escapist hobbies separate. That is to say, I do not drink when I'm fishing. Perhaps because I've developed some pompous notion about the solitude and contemplative nature of fishing, of quiet intrusions and violent battles in natural realms. Perhaps my hunger for the sweet taste of white flesh served with the inner glow of good whiskey is enhanced by thinking I've subdued the flesh sober and honorably. Perhaps the tradition not only of my family but of Hemingway's family and of the others who write of fishing make the two hobbies seem linked in ways I just can't approve. And perhaps the vulgar vision of beer cans rusting on sandy seabeds turns my stomach to the dual endeavor. Perhaps I do not wish to insult the beauty of my aquatic encounters; perhaps I prefer to relish the glow of drink with the memory rather than the experience. Perhaps, because I have become the sort of purist who talks about the difference between outdoor writing and nature writing, I struggle to find my place in that taxonomy and resist the recognition of my own categorization. Perhaps, unlike Lorain Hemingway, I perceive the scene itself more kindly when not viewed through the lens of spirit and the memory of the scene enhanced with the delicate fog of drink. Perhaps my ego is barely tolerable when I'm sober.

But, having said that, let me reiterate: I am a drinker. I am a fan of places where drinking takes place, as long as it doesn't take place on a boat. In my years at Willoughby Bay Marina I witnessed countless accounts of alcohol induced stupidity. I have seen a drunk drive his boat straight up a boat ramp into the parking lot with no trailer or truck waiting to accept the floating fiberglass. I have watched a proud father take his five-year-old son out on their first ever, brand new boat to celebrate the Fourth of July, only to see the crumpled, burned out hull towed back to the dock because he was too drunk to miss the pilings on the bridge. He won't walk again, and he gets to visit his son's grave every Fourth.

I for one am glad to hear that the Coasties and marine police will be increasing their enforcement of laws which make operating a boat while under the influence illegal. As the numbers of boaters and the numbers of boats grows exponentially each year, if we do not do something to make boating safe, more fathers are going to see their children die on the water at the hands of alcohol. In Florida, boat registration nearly tripled between 1970 and 1994. I am amazed that we allow any fool who can pay for a boat to drive one without any sort of training or licensing. There is absolutely no reason why we should not impose stricter laws regarding boats and personal watercraft (personal watercraft, by the way, ought to be banned completely; they are, as James A. Hall writes, "asshole machines"). Licensing tests ought to be imposed for all such crafts. We would never let a fool who paid for an airplane fly it without proper training and licensing, but let a guy buy 4000 pounds of floating fiberglass and steel with 250 horses pushing it and any drunk can drive. I'm not suggesting we deny anyone the right to operate a boat, just that we impose a training system for those who do. It seems logical and safe.

Okay. Before I let my anger carry me into a rant about policing boaters, and before I begin to sound like some teetotalling old biddy, let me return to the subject at hand: alcohol. Like I said, some people have written some great things about alcohol. How about Hemingway who said, "Always do sober what you said you'd do drunk. That will teach you to keep your mouth closed." Good advice. Hemingway also wrote in *For Whom the Bell Tolls*, "An intelligent man is sometimes forced to be drunk to spend time with his fools." Hemingway said a lot about alcohol, probably because he was so often drinking. How about Henny Youngman, who said, "When I read about the evils of drinking, I gave up reading." Funny stuff. Benjamin Franklin: "Beer is proof that God loves us and wants us to be happy." Wise man, that Ben, but I'm guessing he read a bit of Plato, who wrote, "He was a wise man who invented beer." I'm also amazed with the characters in Steinbeck's *Tortilla Flat*. Danny, The Pirate, Pilon, Big Joe, and the rest go through a "gallon of wine" in just about every paragraph. Those boys can do some drinking.

I like writers who aren't afraid to write about drinking. And to admit to it, I like the places where people gather to drink. One of the great things about bars is that some of the absolutely best ones on Earth seem to spring up in places where fisherfolk wander. In fact, there are entire towns that become great places to go to drink namely because there are lots of anglers around. We've all seen the bumper sticker: "A quiet little drinking village with a fishing problem." I've always liked that one, and always looked for places that fit that description. Take for instance the port town of Seward, Alaska, where salmon and halibut fishermen slog about in rubber boots and rain gear. Seward is a town of picture post-card proportions. The harbor is filled with beautiful boats and surrounded with snow-capped mountains. It's a place where one can rent kayaks for ecotours of the bays and glaciers, and one can get a job cleaning salmon in canneries. There are gorgeous stilt homes juxtaposed with tent cities of laborers in town during the canning season. Seward is one of those towns where the adventurous soul can find plenty of adventure and the serene individual can find peace.

I've spent some time there getting acquainted with the bars. By far my favorite is a little place located just down the Old Seward Road on the way out to Lowell Point called the Yukon Bar. The place is planked in old wood with a good solid wood bar with wood benches and stools. Wood makes a bar. I've never been in a bar that was made of formica and steel and glass that was of any use to me. Wood and brass, that's the stuff bars are made of. Bars are as much a condition of wood as they are of drink.

The Yukon Bar proudly boasts the quote "More whiskey and fresh horses for my men" as its motto, which Andrea and Michelle the bartenders tell me was uttered by Alaska Nellie some years back. The Yukon keeps a wheel of cheese by the door from which patrons can chunk off pieces as they please. Its got a pool table and a bandstand and just enough light to keep you from bumping into things. The Yukon is pure bar. The first time I chewed on whiskey there, I decided that it was my kind of place since it was the only bar in town which didn't shut down when a tsunami warning was issued. I'm with the Yukon crowd; if the tsunami is taking Seward, I'm going out with a drink in my hand.

The other great thing about the Yukon is its heads. Bear heads and claws proudly decorate the back of the bar. Propped up above the dusty bottles, two big griz skulls rest among the other Alaska paraphernalia. I've noticed recently that heads and good bars seem to go together; many of my favorite drinking establishments keep heads above the bar: bear heads, boar heads, gator heads, deer heads. I like a place that's got a good head on its bar.

There are no heads in the Salty Dawg Saloon in Homer, Alaska, but that's okay because there aren't many places left like the Salty Dawg. The Salty Dawg occupies the old lighthouse out on Homer Spit. The lighthouse itself is a landmark and has weathered well over a century of storms. The Salty Dawg is a solid wood refuge from the cold and wind and bald eagles that infest the spit much like gulls do on southern beaches. Proprietors John and Lynn Warren know what running a bar is all about. One afternoon, after a day of halibut fishing, I sought refuge in the Salty Dawg from a persistent rain that had been battering my tent for two days. I chanced to meet a gentleman there who informed me that he was moving from Homer to Pepsi Cola, Florida, where he was going to go to bible school. I congratulated him on his acceptance to the school, but informed him that he meant Pensacola. He was adamant that he was going to Pepsi Cola, and when I argued the pronunciation with him he threw a holy roller tantrum which earned him a quick escort out into the rain.

The Salty Dawg is also one of the two only places I've ever been that checked my money to see if it was counterfeit. The second place is Marty and June Arnoldy's Summit Lake Lodge on the Old Seward Highway (around milepost 45.8) just outside of Anchorage at Moose Pass. They serve some great caribou sausage there. I have a friend who used to teach in an Athabascan village in Alaska who tells me that everyone he knew made wine or beer or shine or vodka to get through the Alaskan winters. I suppose that making cash is as profitable a winter pastime as is making hooch. By the way, if you want to set your GPS for quick tracking to the Salty Dawg, it's located at 151° 25′ 10′W and 59° 36′ 9′N.

Though not a bar, there is a place that everyone who visits Alaska ought to be made aware of. It's a small restaurant just outside of Soldotna, Alaska, on the Sterling Highway. It's a simple place that sells pizza, some of the best pizza ever constructed, and some damn fine salads. When I went to Bub's Moose River Pizza the first couple of times, it was owned by Bub Mercier. Bub had an employee, Ray, who is an avid saltwater angler, but not the sort you'd expect to find in Alaska. Ray has an affinity for dolphin and sailfish. He's got a pile of *Saltwater Sportsman*, *Florida Sportsman*, and *Sport Fishing* magazines lying around Bub's, and the place is decorated with pictures of Ray posed with dolphin and other warm water species. It seems that Ray has the same kind of affinity for warm water that I do, and he tries to get down to Florida at least once a year to feed his lust. I understand Ray's longing for warmth and blue water. Somehow Kansas and its lack of water seems so much colder and intolerable than Alaska ever could. At least Ray's got salmon and halibut and grayling and dolly varden. I've got contaminated carp in a flood drain.

I was first introduced to Bub's Moose River Pizza by Ron Martinelli, a dentist from Soldotna, Alaska, who has, as far as I can tell, the perfect life. He has a beautiful wife and kids, a house that would make every man alive drool, and is mere moments from Bub's incomparable pizza. Ron took me and my friend Anis to Bub's after we had been king salmon fishing on the Kenai. Ron, as I learned, is a legend among local fishermen, and his knowledge of the Kenai surpasses that of most guides. I was fortunate that he was hospitable enough to take me out on the Kenai. It seems that Ron has become disgruntled with the overcrowding of his home river, much as the rest of us are tired of the same thing on other rivers around the country, and he's sworn off fishing the Kenai in recent years. In fact, the day he took me out, most of the guides on the river pulled up alongside to say hi and note that it had been years since they'd seen him out on the river. That evening as we gnawed on Bub's first-rate pizza, Ron told me that he and Ray and Bub have a friendly agreement wherein Ron doesn't pay for pizza and Ray and Bub and their families don't pay for dental work. I like that. Neighbors and friends acting like neighbors and friends should. We need more of that. In fact, let me take this opportunity to offer my services as an editor of those cocktail napkins with catchy little phrases printed on them to any restaurant that will let me eat for free each time I come in. I spoke with Ron just the other day, and he told me that Bub sold the Moose River Pizza place, which now calls itself Magpies', but that the pizza is still worth the trip down the Sterling Highway.

Alas, Alaska is not the only place where the drinking and eating are good, though there are many more places which warrant noting in some drinker's guide to Alaska (check out the Great Alaskan Bush Company in Anchorage for starters). Now there's a book I'd volunteer to research and write, or better yet, how about a television show like Ford Division's *Fly Fishing America*; some major corporation could pay me to take off for a year and travel around the country drinking in various bars. They could send a camera crew along to film me drinking Jack Daniels and striking out with women all across the country. I could even add voiceovers like the ones Flip Pallot has on *The Walker's Cay Chronicles*: "As the day started, I dug myself out from the dark twinge of yesterday's show" (close up of Sid's bloodshot eyes). "Did you see the size of that shooter?" I'd even be willing to do a little fishing if they wanted; Ford Division's *Fishing and Drinking America*. I think it has potential. Just think of all of those hungover souls who would roll out of bed on Saturday mornings and tune in *ESPN Outdoors* (or would that be *ESPN Indoors*?) just in time to see me doing what they just did the night before.

I could start the show in those Southern bars where I perfected my art. Places like Skipper's Smokehouse in Tampa, which ranks as not only one of my favorite bars, but one of my all-around favorite places. Skipper's is a fisherman's place, even though it is several miles away from the beach. They serve gator and raw oysters and by far the best grouper sandwich anywhere, despite what other Tampa Bay residents might tell you. They've got a sand pit out back for dancing and a stage where some of the best blues and reggae bands around play nightly. I will admit, in defense of Kansas, that Kansas City (though actually the Missouri portion) is home to some great blues bars, including the Grand Emporium, which in my book is the best blues bar in the country. It's made of wood, has the sort of clientele with whom you'd want to drink, great ribs, and the best music around. Even the blues bars in Chicago, though great in their own respect, don't compare with the Grand Emporium. But, Skipper's gets some of the same acts. And in the middle of the winter, you can still dance barefoot in shorts while worrying about the ice in your drink melting at Skippers. At the Grand Emporium in the winter, outside is no place to be.

Skipper's is without a doubt my favorite, but Tampa has it's share of great places. Take for instance, The Hub, where drinks are poured in water glasses and you feel guilty paying so little for them. The Hub is not for the weak drinker. People only go to the Hub for one reason: a debilitating drunk. If you're in Tampa and someone simply says "Hub" to you, brace yourself. But if you want the drinker's tour of Tampa, just go to Ybor City on a Saturday night. Ybor City puts New Orleans' Mardi Gras to shame on an average Saturday night, and all with a pirate's flair. Don't get me wrong, of course; New Orleans is another of those Southern cities that makes an angler feel at home, particularly an angler with a taste for whiskey and seafood.

Now, I can ramble along about bars and cities and places worth visiting simply based upon their drinking establishments, but doing so seems more an activity for my own nostalgia than for the discussions of alcohol and fishing. As I began by saying, I am intrigued by the enmeshing of these two escapist hobbies. For many of us, myself included, fishing is an activity that gives us moment to think about the important stuff, to find ourselves, to find the spirit in ourselves and in the world which lets us exhale our burdens and inhale the fresh air of living. I'm often amazed at the individuals I see fishing who are perpetually angry with the whole activity—people who curse the boat and their luck, their tackle and their partners. Certainly, we have all had several of those days when everything goes wrong on a fishing outing, but I'm speaking of the individuals we have all seen who seem to be more bitter about the event than relaxed. Every exhale pounces out amidst curses and frustration; the inhales are laced with a vile disdain for the day. That's not what fishing is about.

Nor is that what drinking is about. As adamant as I am that fishing be a time of contented relaxation, so too am I strict about how drinking gets done. The spirit of the spirit is crucial. We've all seen bad drunks, and we've seen drunks who are bad. But that pleasant fog of lacquered haze can be such an uplifting drink. Imagine the warmth of a whiskey before the taste of good meat, the glow of a wine just as you settle into a comfortable chair, the coolness of a beer just after you brush your teeth in the morning; that's the good stuff. And for me, there is also the company that happens when drinking happens. As it often happens, some of my best drinking takes place around the people I like the best, or that I'm just getting to like.

My drinking has evolved a lot like my fishing. I've never tried to deny my taste for either, but early on I was not very good at either. When I was younger, I was an impatient angler. My brothers used to make fun of my fishing style: I would run frantically to whatever spot another angler had just caught a fish and cast to that spot until another angler caught a fish, at which time I'd run to that spot and crowd that angler. I also used to be one of those fishermen who would spend most of the day angry and frustrated; I would throw my gear away in anger when the fish didn't hit. Luckily, I grew out of that; I have become complacent. I am as content to stand without the rod and reel and watch the Picassoesque swirls of the water or the charge of the mullet. I take new pleasures in fishing, in being in the places where fishing happens, in the honor of the fish's fight and the humbleness of its surrender. Similarly, I am relaxed in those places where drinking happens. I no longer feel the need to boast my prowess in quantity nor attempt to exceed my last outing. The amateur angler and drinker are similar in this vein: each think that more is better. When I was in high school we used to say the same thing about a freshly opened beer as we would about a just-landed fish: "kill it."

Now don't hear my curmudgeonly wisdom of drinking to be a proclamation of drinking snobbery. Worse than anything is a pompous drinker, a beer snob, a connoisseur. What I disdain is the drinker who refuses to drink a Budweiser because "Americans just don't know how to make beer." So move to Germany. I was sitting in some bar somewhere between Georgia and Tennessee when the guy next to me called the bartender over to complain that the nitrogen mix in his draft beer was obviously off since the bubbles were flowing to the top of his brew at entirely too rapid a rate. This is not a drinker; this is a prick. Three years ago I was invited to interview for a teaching position at American University in Washington, D.C. During the two days of interviews, I was to be the guest at a dinner at a faculty member's home. The entire evening was spent listening to our host tell stories of each bottle of wine in his cellar as though he were talking about rare paintings and as though the rest of us were uneducated twits. Prick. I've walked out of countless bars when informed "we don't serve domestics," and I've stayed in countless more simply to argue the logic of such statements.

It's not that I have any objection to people being interested in their drinks, in becoming experts. In fact, I think it's pretty cool. It's the individuals, though, who pass judgement on the rest of us because we don't appreciate the expensive stuff that ticks me off. It's the same sort of purism with which dry-fly anglers look down their noses at bait fishermen. Granted, I may seem a bit hypocritical here as I grasp my own devotions with as much religious fervor as the next guy, but I can live with contradictions. I wish I knew about wines, about beers, about specialty whiskeys. But the fact is, I like American beers and whiskeys. Only once in the history of human kind has any judgement of another individual based on their drink preference been at all reasonable, and that occurred when the great Southern philosopher Lewis Grizzard proclaimed, "Never trust a man who drinks see-through whiskey." I consider this one of the most profound assessments of gin and vodka drinkers, who tend to be used car salesmen, real estate agents, lawyers, and men who wear Italian loafers. I'm willing to bet that you won't find a gin or vodka drinker in the automotive section of Walmart or in a fly shop. Unfortunately, you can often find them driving boats.

On the Fly

I've been thinking a lot about fly fishing recently. That is, I've been reading a lot about fly fishing and thinking about how fly fishing gets written. I'm not much of a flyfisherman myself; I've really just started learning. But, I am beginning to see that the publishing industry has taken note of fly fishing to the tune of countless books and magazines. I'm glad for this. I've found some wonderful books by eloquent authors who are able to write the graceful art of fly-casting into the pages of books in ways that make the reading as much fun as the casting.

But, I must also confess, I'm beginning to have some suspicions about the literature of fly fishing. I'm beginning to detect hints of religious fervor which seek to convert anglers to the honest activity of the fly. I often feel myself captured by the spell of the pastoral settings, the innocence of the fly, and the purity of the fly rod. I've even started buying fly rods, both freshwater and saltwater, though my experiences with them have been limited. My fishing partner Roy berates me whenever I begin talking about fly rodding. He calls them "fairy wands" and pretty much loathes what he perceives as a pompous attitude that gets associated with the devotion to the fly rod—he gripes about anglers of the fly much like I rant about beer and wine snobs.

I've had a hard time with his resistance because I too find myself not wanting my fishing to become elitist. When I first started to write for fishing magazines my goal was to provide hints about tackle and locations for anglers who could not afford the big-money tackle and resort spots often touted as what one must have or where one must go in order to be a real angler. To me, fishing isn't about expensive tackle and exotic locales; it is about being alone near water and trying to catch fish. But in reading all I have about fly fishing, perhaps more so than in my reading about marlin fishing or offshore boats or other high-finance aspects of angling, I've begun to fall prey to the majesty depicted about fly fishing ; there is an innocence and perfection about it which is captivating.

I've been writing about this lately, writing about fly fishing, thinking about fly fishing, but not really thinking about why it's become central to my thoughts on fishing. I suppose that in addition to all of the Gierach, Traver, Lyons, and other fly rod writers I've been reading, I've been out here in Kansas closer to the rivers where flyfishing gets done in books and farther from the waters where I learned to fish. I've had to adjust my thinking from salt water to fresh water, and not really knowing what that means, I've fallen prey to a fantasy constructed by writers. I guess I've wanted to make myself part of a fishing culture that gets branded "serious fisherman" out here, just as an offshore angler or tarpon fisherman might wear the badge of serious fisherman in Florida. In the Midwest and regions west and north of Kansas, trout become the quest for those who wear this badge.

As I've said, I grew up fishing, but my fishing was not trout fishing. Well, that's not exactly true; I've certainly caught my share of specks, grays, silvers, and other saltwater trout. But that's not what people mean by "trout fishing." That's certainly not what Traver, Wulff, McLean, Gierach, Lyons, or Raymond mean by trout fishing. That's how I learned about *real* trout fishing: books and magazines. I inhale books, articles, and stories about fishing as fast as I can, and it seems that most of them paint pictures of trout fishing. So, that's how I learned. Sitting on porches or docks or beaches overlooking the blue expanses of the Atlantic or the Gulf of Mexico or the Chesapeake Bay or Tampa Bay, and now out here away from those places, I drink in page after page of this beautiful and foreign thing called trout fishing. I learned about the hierarchies that exist: bait fishermen are scavengers and fly fishermen are artists. And even there I learned about dry-fly purists and split-bamboo purists. My vision of the artist grew; my vision of noble battles on cold, flowing rivers grew; my vision of rugged sportsmen huddled in fire-lit cabins on winter days tying delicate flies and staring at their creations in the flicker of light, drinking old whiskey, and floating in dreams of the trout whose mouth would sip in that particular fly still drying in the vise. And my dream-vision of the trout grew: majestic creatures endowed with the strength and intelligence to make them the most honorable game, and more beautiful than dreams themselves. These romanticized images of trout fishing grew.

I even started doubting my own fishing. Before leaving Florida, I gave up bait and moved strictly to artificials. And I loved it. Even before I left my salt waters, I felt that I was somehow moving up that mythical ladder of anglers where trout fishermen sit supreme, and the redfish and snook that I released were somehow more honorably taken since I was now several rungs up as a sportsman—that a better fisherman was somehow catching better fish in better ways. Lighter tackle, lighter leaders, releasing more fish, reveling in each catch more and more. I was converted.

Trout fishing, the pinnacle of my fisherman's image, may have been beyond my geographical reach then, but I was following in spirit. When last in Florida, I even bought an eight-and-a-half-foot, seven weight fly rod and carried it on every expedition. I frustrated myself trying to learn to cast big saltwater patterns—streamers, deceivers, crazy charlies, Stu Apte tarpon flies—in rough surf or on choppy flats. I asked my editors for casting lessons. It was clear that saltwater fly fishing was rapidly becoming the trout fishing of the saltwater world, and I wanted in. I even fished with anglers who wouldn't allow spinning tackle on their boats—fly or nothing. Purists evolved. I tossed flies at tarpon, permit, and bonefish in the Keys, redfish and snook up and down Florida's west coast, and never did a fish even look my way. In desperation, I always moved back to spinning gear; at least I knew I could catch fish. I managed to forget to reach for that whippy seven weight even when the bluefish were churning up the surf of North Carolina's Outer Banks mere feet from where I stood on the shore. No casting. Just lay a streamer out in front of me, and surely, surely I could claim to have caught fish on the fly. But it was always too hard to break myself from the excitement of a good blue run—where just about every cast locks you into a solid fight with a piranha of the Atlantic—and run back up the beach to grab that fly rod. Besides, the frenzy might end before I'd get back, and catching fish on a Hopkins spoon is certainly catching fish. But still, just once, I should have grabbed that fly rod and moved one more step up that ladder. Sure, catching fish is catching fish, but a fisherman who takes a fish on a fly—that's *real* fishing.

Career moves took me from my oceans and straight to the Midwest. My grandfather told me to practice my casting because even with my 15-foot surf rod, clearing that second breaker would be a bear when casting from Kansas. Everyone who knew me wanted to know what I'd do to sate my hunger for fishing in the Midwest. "Not too many snook in Kansas" they told me. But the job was just too good to pass by. Besides, Kansas is the Midwest, and the Midwest breeds trout fishermen. Geographically, I was one step closer to joining the others on those upper rungs.

The way I figured it, Missouri was right next door, the Ozarks a mere three-hour drive, and that meant that trout fishing was in reach. I had even read about trout fishing at Crane Creek, an easy weekend trip from Lawrence. I made sure my new home had a fireplace and a great room for tying flies on those days that found me snow bound. Adding good whiskey to complete the picture was easy enough. I was going to jump headlong into the upper echelon of sportsmen. I may not have had the years of experience on rivers, but I was willing—perhaps even eager—to be as curmudgeonly and stubborn as I had to be in order to pass myself off as one of the ranking royalty. I had already taken to grumbling about the commercialism that had pillaged outdoorsmanship, particularly fishing, and especially fly fishing. To me a truck will always be a truck, not a "sport utility vehicle," and ordering all of your clothes from L.L. Bean or Cabella's does not make one a sportsman. I had also, with true conviction, dedicated myself to conservation and environmental concerns. I may not have been a TU member, but I joined IGFA and collected signatures for Florida's SOS campaign. My heart was in the right place, and I knew I'd be good at being a trout fisherman.

So I caught my first trout. And I owe the trout fishermen—the ones who *really* sit atop that ladder—an apology.

I hadn't held a rod in my hand or wet a line in the four months since I moved. November brought the first dusting of snow to east Kansas, and the local paper brought news of a nearby trout lake. This was it; I was going to make my move into trout fishing. But as soon as I purchased my trout license, I realized I was a fraud. I knew instantly that even if I stood complacently by my favorite spot on a secret river, warming my hands on the bowl of a freshly lit pipe as snow fell and I watched native browns rise before me and I contemplated which of the flies I'd tied the night before would be best to cast out with my split-bamboo rod, I'd never be more than one of the thousands of wanabees answering the romantic call-of-the-trout forwarded by the same books I'd locked into my soul. I'd have been called a "hoe-dad" or a "poser" by the surfers back home had I tried to step into their world in the same way.

But I wasn't willing to give up. I advanced slowly. I explored the local outdoor shops and again and again heard the same two short sentences: "Fishing's over, boy. It's time to hunt." And those who would talk fishing looked at me sort of cockeyed: "Not too many people flyfish around here. You need to go to Arkansas or Missouri for that." But this actually inspired me, made me seem like sort of a misfit in the local outdoor scene, almost eccentric. Maybe I would fit in as an eccentric fly fisherman after all. But this crazy thought kept crossing my mind: in all of my reading, why couldn't I remember any of those mystical fly-fishing types writing about Kansas as a worthy place in which to practice the art?

So when the skies cleared a little, I made my way to the trout lake. Not knowing much about lakes (other than to check for gators before wading in), I approached this small public lake and asked myself, "At what point does a lake become a pond, or a pond a puddle?" This lake, like all lakes in Kansas as I have learned, was man-made—there are no natural lakes in Kansas. My first impression of this three-acre, arrowhead-shaped mud puddle was not the same impression that trout fishermen in the books had when they first came upon the north fork of some famous river or another. But I was going trout fishing.

Now I must offer my apology to those atop the ladder, not for falling in love with the romantic image so well painted by writers of the trout fisherman and his art, but for disobeying every single cardinal law one must obey in order to take a seat in the ranks of trout fishermen that this very image champions.

I had chosen this particular lake to begin my career as a trout fisherman for the simple reason that the newspaper had announced that it had been stocked with 400 rainbow trout earlier in the week. There was no careful exploration to find a quiet fork of a river that held a promising looking beaver dam; there was no hope of finding wild brookies rising to some unseen hatch. I know now, and knew then, that fishing for anything but wild trout is not fishing for trout, and that I, by not doing so, placed my name on the blackball list of all legitimate trout fishermen. In many places, I'm sure that I would not be allowed to even order a Budweiser in a local tavern should this crime become public. "We don't serve your kind here."

I walked around this lake learning to read the water—a task I expected to be much different from learning to read the flats of Tampa Bay or the deep water of the Middle Grounds. I found that there wasn't a spot out of the reach of my ultra-light outfit's cast. Sadly, the high winds kept me from even trying my impotent fly casting, and the seven weight rested in the grass as I continued to fall even further from grace. Granted, casting the seven-weight here would have been equivalent to jigging for mangrove snapper with a tuna rod. I stood on the muddy banks casting into this small pond filled with 400 farm-raised fish, and I felt embarrassed, half afraid someone might catch me cheating my way into the trout club. Weeks before I had been hiking and camping in South Dakota with one of my best friends and adventuring partners when we came across a place called "Trout Haven" where one could pay a fee to fish in a ditch full of farm-raised trout. "Guaranteed" to catch fish the sign informed us. I cursed and made a big to-do that such a place was even allowed to use the word "fishing." But when I went trout fishing, I stood casting to essentially a public version of that abomination.

As I stood there casting, I found myself drifting to that place where casting becomes an involuntary action like a heartbeat or deep-sleep breathing. I found my mind lost in the surroundings: the last bit of snow was melting in the grass and around the leafless trees; a whitetail deer had moved to the other side of the lake to drink and then run off at a sound audible to it and not to me; other small animals dashed by, leaving me with no concrete glimpse, just wonders of what kind of animal that was running behind the tree line. My eyes stared lackadaisically at the small black snake that was inspecting my net as it lay carelessly tossed to the browned grass on the fringes of the remaining snow. And all of this time, my casting never missed a beat. Though I consciously forgot that I was casting, my form returned, and I effortlessly pitched a small gold Kastmaster spoon to the center of the lake where it landed with a light "plip" time and time again. My mind had begun to take comfort in being in that place— that zone—again after so many months away.

As I drifted around in that place, I felt a small thud in my rod hand. "Hey, dummy, that's a fish," my brain hollered at me to bring me back. And sure enough, it was. A small, farm-raised, stocked rainbow trout had placed all three points of my small treble hook in its mouth, and on the Olympus of the fly-fishing gods, my name was written and sealed in an ever-growing blacklist.

This small trout had none of the glorious color I expect-ed it to have. It barely stretched from the end of my thumb to the tip of my little finger. Its body felt mushy, not firm and muscular like a mackerel or tuna or bluefish. Its snubbed face looked weak and unintelligent. There was no aggression, no attempt to win freedom, just stunned surrender. The fish that I had expected to live up to those written images—to be cunning, strong, intelligent, and worthy game—was soft, weak, small, and pathetic. I felt ill looking at it. I sinned against all that fly fishing in its purist form was represented in the words of books and essays to be. And as I stood there in the mud, this trout died. There was no glory of the release, no final redemption. I'm not sure if the little thing was too weak to survive until release, or if I was the weak one.

I'll fly to Virginia for Thanksgiving this year like all years. I'll spend a few days in North Carolina bluefishing and a day or so out on the Chesapeake Bay striper fishing, but I won't be carrying a fly rod. For whatever explanation one chooses to attribute to it—fate, God's punishment, bad luck, plain old coincidence—I accidentally slammed that seven-weight fly rod in the truck tailgate as I left that "lake" in Kansas. It's downstairs by the fireplace, broken, having never caught any fish, let alone a trout. I have several rods I've "retired" for various reasons. This is the first I'll keep as a reminder of my transgressions against what writers present as a beautiful, honest sport. I'm not sure how long I'll be in the Midwest, and I'm not sure when I'll buy a new fly rod and try again. But for now I do know that I broke that rod, and I broke faith. Perhaps I trespassed in a realm of fishing where I just don't belong, where initiations of faith are life-long devotions, not weekend conversions.

So, the fact remains, I am not much of a flyfisherman, though since my transgressions against the trout world, I decided to try again, this time in more familiar salt waters while back at the cottage in Kitty Hawk. As it became more and more evident that the movie version of *A River Runs Through It* had created a conventional wisdom that dictates that if you don't fly fish, you don't fish, I decided I had better try again to hop on the bandwagon fast if I was to retain any reputation as a fisherman. But, as I have said, it turns out that I am just not very good at this graceful sport. So in the year since that day in Kansas, I've made a concerted effort to cast flies at salmon and grayling in Alaska; at tarpon, permit, and bonefish in the Keys; and at wild and stocked trout in various lakes and rivers all over the lower 48 (I've taken to traveling to fishing spots outside of Kansas as often as possible—thank God for the academic's life). But, the truth is, even to this day, I've never caught anything over 20 pounds on the fly.

"Nothing over 20 pounds?" you ask; "that leaves room for some damn big fish!" But the real truth is, I haven't taken anything under twenty pounds either, not really. Plain and simple, until recently, I had never landed a single fish on the fly, though I did have one land-locked silver salmon grab a fly on a Kenai peninsula lake in Alaska. Unfortunately, I was so baffled as to what to do once it grabbed the fly, and I was so busy pointing and yelling to my companions, "Damn thing actually hit it!" that I never got around to setting the hook, and the salmon figured if I was too stupid to set the hook then it didn't want any part of me.

The problem here is not that I cannot catch fish on the fly—there are lots of people who can't. The problem is that I write about fishing and I cannot catch fish on the fly. After the popularity of *A River Runs Through It* and books like *Fly Fishing Through the Mid-Life Crisis* capped the best-seller list, it seems that if one wishes to write about fishing it has to be about the noble art of fly fishing. Even my students want to write dissertations on fly fishing. As I've said, current thinking has created a hierarchy that places fly fishing atop the sportsman ladder. The numbers of books on store shelves that extol the virtues of the fly fisherman's art, particularly if that angler hunts wild trout, have clearly defined what contemporary fishing is all about. Bookstores carry few titles about saltwater fishing (other than how-to books), let alone saltwater fishing that doesn't mention fly rods. Of course, authors like Stu Apte and Mark Sosin are able to place an occasional essay about saltwater fly fishing in anthologies, but American readers are less likely to purchase books on catching tarpon, blues, stripers, or snook than collections of stories about wild brown trout. (Less likely, but not altogether resistant. There are some good books and authors out there—and readers too.) That makes my life as an outdoor writer even more difficult since I haven't heard of many wild brown trout being taken in any of the salt water where I like to do my fishing, and editors keep telling me they won't print fly-fishing stories that are about *not* catching fish (besides, Nick Lyons has already made a career of writing those stories).

Now I know I have missed many an opportunity to actually catch a fish on the fly because of my own stubbornness. There have been dozens of times during Outer Banks summers when the tailor blues were hitting in the surf so close to my feet that I would not actually have had to cast the fly; I could have simply dangled a streamer into the surf and made the claim: "Yep, I've taken blues on the fly." But when fish are hitting jigs, there's little chance that I'll be running up the beach to get a fly rod—after all, *the fish are hitting*. But, as luck would have it, and as so much of my fishing education has occurred on the Outer Banks, I got my first fish on the fly this summer while back at the Kitty Hawk cottage.

Surf casting action had been about what it usually is in late July on the Outer Banks: good runs of spot, some flounder around, scattered Spanish and small blues, rumors of kings off the ends of the piers, but the ends of piers were so crowded that you wouldn't want to be there anyway. So, in my usual stay-away-from-crowds manner, I decided that I would take a few afternoon hours to practice my fly casting just in case the opportunity would arise anytime soon that I might need those casting skills that I so thoroughly lacked. I put on wading shoes, grabbed the whippy five weight with which I replaced the broken seven weight and with which I feel most comfortable, tied on a green and white streamer, and headed on to the flats behind the Oregon Inlet Fishing Center. I like wading back there under the bridge, but I have to admit, I don't catch many fish there anymore. The shifting sands of the inlet have changed the topography so much over the years that knowing "the spots" in the shallows of the inlet is near impossible, and as most of us who fish there have come to recognize, the whole inlet just does not produce like it used to. So, I figured that the day was just a day to practice casting and to wade around in the warm waters with the crabs.

I wandered back around the bridge toward the point, watching small schools of baitfish, crabs, birds, and the other inhabitants of the tidal waters. All the while, I shot that streamer out in less than artistic roll casts, and I beat the water both in front of me and behind me to a froth. Since it took too much concentration on my behalf to actually cast the line without fault, I was unable to enjoy the peaceful, rhythmic motion of casting, and instead I became frustrated—a sensation for which I go fishing in order to escape. But as my persistence would have it, I occasionally managed to lay that streamer out in front of me with some resemblance of competence.

On one such cast, as I was congratulating myself for casting farther than 10 feet and was stripping the line back toward me, a flounder grabbed the streamer. When we fish, no matter how slow a day of fishing it is, we always tend to have at least a slight expectation that something could possibly hit our lines, so in even the most minute way, we are prepared to react. I was not. In my mind, I had gone out there to practice casting, not to go fishing. The flounder that had hit the fly was obviously not aware of my agenda, so it took the streamer anyway.

Unlike the silver salmon mishap, I managed to set the hook this time—not because I had refined my skill to where I knew how to react, but because I was so taken off guard by the actual idea that a fish had struck my fly that I lifted the rod tip in basic startled reaction. Unfortunately, this reaction would not have effectively set the hook except for the fact that I had carelessly tangled the line around the reel spool, causing the line to tighten and set the hook. After that, I had little choice but to pull the fish in, which I did without having to fight him down to the backing more than twice—not because the fighting prowess of a 14-inch flounder is such that he could strip my reel to the backing, but because I couldn't figure out how to get the line to evenly spool, this being my first fight with a fish on the fly and all. So I was twice forced to unwind and try again.

I released that flounder in true fly-fisherman style. I'm still convinced that I'll never figure out the coordination of fly fishing, which will probably hinder my career as an outdoor writer, but I figure if the sequel to *A River Runs Through It* contains at least one scene with an Outer Banks flounder, it will be a much better movie.

Industry

I have been lucky. I have stood with my nose mere inches from some of the world's most beautiful paintings. I have stared endlessly at the brush strokes of Bellini, Klee, Rembrandt, Cezanne, Van Gogh, Gauguin, Manet, Renoir, Degas, Monet, Rousseau, Matisse, Picasso, Toulouse-Lautrec, Dali, Wyeth, O'Keefe, and Chagall. I have found solace in the waves of their colors much like I have in the waves of salt water. I have become lost in the curves and angles and dimension of sculptures by Rodin, Lehmbruck, Moore, Boccioni, Brancusi, Remington, and Giacometti. I have stood before the architectural wonders of Teotihuacan, London Bridge, Sears Tower, the Golden Gate Bridge, the Wallace Monument. I have stood at Rhodes where the golden

Colossus stood. I have listened to symphonies play the music of Mozart, Wagner, and Beethoven; and I have heard the live music of the Allman Brothers, Stevie Ray Vaughn, Koko Taylor, Professor Longhair, and a host of Delta blues artists who know how to blend guitars, pianos, and hot sauce. I have seen mountains and rivers and plains and valleys in sun and rain and snow and storm. And though experiencing these wonders of human and nature have been moving, nothing compares to the beauty and wonder and sound of salt water.

I fall in love with blue water each time my eyes fall upon it. "Love"—an interesting choice here. It would be easy to compare the works of art, the sculptures, the nature to the love for a woman, or even for God. But in my life, blue water has more often than not held captive my heart more than any woman and is where I go to be close to God.

There is something remarkably spiritual about the world, about the natural wild places where I roam. My dear friend Rob has always contended that I am a spiritual person, but until recently I was not sure what he meant by that. On days when the human world becomes overbearing, when job, and news, and traffic, and bills, and the pressure of life become too much, I want to be free from all of that. I want to feel the breath of the wind and the spray of the water. I want to touch the world and feel its spirit. Concrete and glass and steel suffocate the spirit; I can't feel life in a building. Perhaps that's why I like wooden bars and wooden piers, because there's still something natural about carving out a place in the wood.

For certain this is why I crave salt water. There is nothing more spiritual, nothing closer to God than the echo of salt water, the space of sea. There is an old saying of which my friends who are surfers often remind me: "Waiting for waves is okay. Most people spend their whole lives waiting for nothing." Life begins in the sea, and it is there I feel the touch of life. Some find that same spirit in the chilled mountain air, in the scent of a conifer forest, in the brush of a desert breeze, in the crash of rams' horns, in the rush of a cold-water creek. These are the places that so many of us go to worship.

As I have said before, when I am confused or lonely or in need of solace, I find comfort in salt water. How I miss all of that out here in the plains. How often I look to the hawks in the sky wishing I could take wing with them and ride the breeze to the sea. And how often I stand in the rain, tasting its wetness, feeling its touch, trying to pull the memory of its last time in the sea and the promise that it will again find its way back to the oceans, wanting to follow it on its journey, wanting to be reunited with salt water.

This is part of the reason why I am so addicted to fishing. There is an old saying, *Piscator non solum piscatur*, which means "fishing is not just about catching fish." For those of us who have moved beyond seeing it as merely about filling coolers with flesh, fishing is the opportunity to taste the water, to find one's place in the world. There are many days when "going fishing" is more about setting the rod aside and just drifting about in the world. There are days when I find more thrill in watching porpoise, and birds, and crabs, and rays, and sharks, and otters than I do in reeling in fish. There are days when the colors and motions of the water and sky are more captivating than casting. And there are days when I am more content to watch schools of feeding blues, or cruising reds, or churning jacks and am most fulfilled to revel in having had the opportunity to witness these wonders. And, of course, always in that pleasure is the spirit of the place, the magic of being in the world.

Also in that moment is the undercurrent that I will never have the opportunities to see the wild world the same way my parents and grandparents did. Nor, I fear, will my children (should I ever be blessed with that joy) see what I saw because more glass and concrete and steel will be needed to accommodate their world. And so, as I am lost in the spirit of fishing, the baggage of what fishing now also includes makes me want for more of that very spirit.

As much as I don't want to have to admit that it's happened, once in a while I have to acknowledge that fishing is no longer an honest sport. It is no longer about survival; it is no longer about nature; it is no longer about innocence. Fishing has become industry, and in this country, industry, while claiming to have improved the sport of angling, has, in fact, begun to corrupt the most contemplative of pastimes. I have been lucky (or not) to have seen a lot of the industry that surrounds fishing, and I will concede there are many good people working in it. People who mean well, who care about protecting fish and environment, people who are committed to the art of angling. But, when all of these good people begin competing for their place at the table where tackle manufacturers, guides, custom rod builders, boat builders, resort managers, fly tiers, and so on push and shove to grab what they can of the cash so many of us are willing to toss to companies to improve our angling, then we fishermen have begun to emphasize the wrong part of fishing. Unfortunately, we have misinterpreted *Piscator non solum piscatur* to mean that fishing is also about cashing in.

Don't hear me wrong. I too enjoy placing large orders through Cabella's, Offshore Angler, and Murray Brothers. I would pay handsomely for a huge offshore fishing machine that bears the name Mako or Pro-Line or Dusky or Contender. I love my Fin-Nor reels and my Yozuri lures. I subscribe to *Saltwater Sportsman*, *Florida Sportsman*, *Field and Stream*, *Sports Afield*, *Flyfishing in Salt Water*, *Gulf Coast Angler*, *The Sportfishing Report*, and a host of other magazines—the very vehicle through which the industry reaches countless anglers and their money. That is not to say, of course, that the publishers, editors, and writers are necessarily money-grubbing fishing elitists. Karl Wickstrom, publisher of *Florida Sportsman*, for instance, is a true fisherman who would be as happy fishing with a hand line, bobber, and worms as he would in an expensive custom boat. Also, Wickstrom has probably done more to help preserve natural marine environments and fisheries than just about anyone around. He is a fine example of what is right with the industry.

Of course, my money feeds directly into this industry, and I hope even by writing these pages to find a place in that industry. So, perhaps what I'm going to say here may seem hypocritical, but recognizing such contradictions in our own lives makes finding the right place on which to stand that much easier. That is, we all live with contradictions; we must at minimum be conscious of them.

There is little doubt that I would love to learn the art of building my own rods. After all, my grandfather and his brother built their own rods; I have friends who build their own rods. I could learn this skill, and I would guess that catching fish on rods I built would somehow seem more noble, more honest. The thrill of the catch would seem that much more mine, that much more personal. But the reality is that Starr and Ocean Master and Penn and G. Loomis make some damn fine rods, as does a host of other large manufacturers and small custom rod shops. So, I'll pay for my gear like the rest of us.

But the industry of fishing exceeds rod building and fly tying and lure making and all other aspects of tackle to the tune of a multibillion-dollar-a-year industry. Publication advertisements, boat companies, guiding, bait catching, piers, charters, marine electronics, clothing, artwork, jewelry, books, videos—the list is as vast as the sea. This is a damn big industry for such a simple pastime. When Izaak Walton or Dame Juliana Berners wrote about fishing, there wasn't this much to it. It was simple. You fished and you either caught fish or not, and you were thankful for being in places where fishing happens. Now you plan and pack and watch weather reports and gauge tides and moons and order gear and rig boats and then fish, and if you don't catch anything you blame bad guides, wrong lures, visible line, overfishing, spoiled water, poor electronics. Bad luck has just gotten too complicated.

Don't get me wrong here, I love the gadgets. I love GPS and fishfinders and autopilot. I love high-visibility line and daisy chains and acrylic lures. But more than anything, I love fishing and would gladly do it with just a bamboo pole, a length of thread, and an old safety pin, just the way my mother used to fish when she was a little girl living in north Florida.

When I first started writing about fishing, I knew precisely why I wanted to do so: because I love fishing and I wanted to share that with others. I wanted to write about the things that I love to read about. I wanted to be a part of the fishing industry in a different way. But the more I read about fishing, the more I realized that many of the same sorts of things were being said about the sport over and over again. I didn't want to fall into the same mode and try to imitate any of the other writers who had made names for themselves. I didn't want to be a bad version of McLean or Gierach; I didn't want to try to mimic Vic Dunaway or George Poveromo. These, and other writers, are some of my favorites, but they've already carved out their niches, and I didn't want to ride on their coat tails.

So, when I asked Andy Dear and Jody Moore of *The Fisherman* how they got to be writers of fishing, I also proposed my idea about what I wanted to write. I wanted to write about the industry and how those of us who couldn't afford the kinds of fishing we see depicted in full-color photographs in the big magazines could fish in beautiful places with less-expensive gear and still catch big fish. After all, despite the attraction of the gizmos, of the custom-built tackle, of the big fiberglass boats, catching fish is still ultimately about one person and one fish. And no matter what links those two together, no matter what attracts the two to the moment of interaction, no matter what luck or timing, fishing is fishing. So I wanted to write to those of us who couldn't afford what was professed to be the good stuff, because the good stuff was already there in the water and the fish and the moment.

At the time, I was in graduate school living on English department stipends, and most of my gear was purchased at flea markets or handed down from my grandfather or father. I had worked in a marina, seen how boats were built and sold, watched how guides worked, how head boats were run, worked at large boat shows. I had begun to see the industry from the inside. I wanted to provide access to the masses who couldn't afford the industry in its gelcoated glory.

I say "gelcoated" here perhaps out of guilt and as an odd segue. I wanted to write for the masses (the fishing socialist it would seem. "Teach a man to fish...") perhaps out of guilt. Not guilt for something I had done, but out of familial guilt, guilt for my grandfather. I say "guilt" sort of half-heartedly. Ultimately, there is no guilt in what I'm going to convey here. In fact there is pride, with a hint of guilt for what has evolved. Since I've never heard another version of this story, and since I want it to be true, I will tell it as such, as truth. It is family legend, and should be Florida legend, American legend. It is part of my pride.

In 1942 my grandfather, Milton Dobrin, was living in Jacksonville, Florida (where he resides to this day and probably knows more about fishing the Mayport area than just about any other living soul). Long before I was born, my grandfather had been a taxi driver; he ran movie houses; he and my grandmother owned and ran a coffee house called the Jongleur, which featured acts included Joan Baez, Steve Martin, Jose Feliciano, and the likes. The fliers I have from the Jongleur days boast it "Jacksonville's only Coffee House (1514 Miami Road)" (the business cards I have from then also say "Jacksonville's finest Coffee House"). He played semiprofessional football; he tried out for the Olympics as a speed skater. He was an ax thrower, and he won best of breed at Westminister Kennel Club for one of his terriers. In 1972 I watched my grandfather graduate from college at Jacksonville University. He wore his black cap and gown and a pair of

Chuck Taylor tennis shoes and a peace sign on his gown. He later became a high school math teacher. And, in the early 1940s my grandfather invented the molded fiberglass boat.

As he tells it, he had been fooling around with different fiberglass molds for small household constructions: sinks, bathtubs, and such. He and his brother, who fished commercially out of Mayport, decided to build a mold big enough for a fiberglass hull. Once the mold was completed, they contacted DuPont to see about getting enough chemicals to mix the resin. DuPont officials, worried about what all the chemicals were being used for, sent representatives down to Jacksonville. According to my grandfather, they stuck around to learn how to use the resin and the molds. Eventually, G'pa successfully built a fiberglass hull, patented the idea, and started a boat company called "Glascraft"—he and my father still think the name is deeply clever. It was the first company to manufacture and sell molded fiberglass boats. However, soon the Navy got word of all of the resin chemicals being shipped to Jacksonville and got curious. The Department of the Navy sent their own representatives down, and upon seeing the operation offered to purchase the company and the patent. And though the Navy sent the same negotiator who wrangled the Indians out of Manhattan for a song, my grandfather accepted their offer and sold the patent for molded fiberglass boats to the Navy for peanuts and turned down a job as an engineer overseeing the process.

As massive as the fiberglass boat industry has become, I know this is a little hard to believe. But I believe it. I know I could, with a little effort, track the patent records, contact DuPont, or search Navy records. I've even begun a patent search a couple of times. But patent data from the 40s is tough to find; local patent offices didn't keep great records all of the time. And besides, I'm not sure I want to find out that he didn't really do all of this, though I've heard the story so many times since I was a kid that I can't not believe it.

So, I want to be sure that everyone who steps on to a fiberglass boat, that everyone who sells these boats, everyone who flips through magazines and lusts after these boats, all of you at Pro-Line, Mako, Bertram, Donzi, Grady-White, Ranger, Aquasport, Dusky, Bayliner, Chris-Craft, and the rest know that my grandfather Milton Dobrin invented the molded fiberglass boat. I want to place my family name in the history of the sport fishing industry, but I want to note the contradiction here as well. Fiberglass boats directly contribute to many of the environmental problems threatening the very places we go to fish. In the late 1980s, for instance, it was discovered that the bottom paints used to protect fiberglass hulls were leeching toxins into salt water, and companies like Petit were forced to find new formulas for their paint. And, of course, the reliability of fiberglass construction provided the boat industry with the materials that could supply the growing demand for pleasure boats. The sheer numbers of boats on the water today accounts for a variety of problems.

But, as I said, I have to live with this contradiction, and I know that as soon as the chance arises, I will own fiberglass boats—not boat, but boats, plural. I enjoy standing barefooted on a white gelcoat deck warmed by the sun and washed in the spray of salt water. I like the sound of water gliding under the hull. I find perfection in the lines of hulls and gunwales and transoms and decks. I like the sound of a scrub brush on a fiberglass deck, and I like the way they clean up white and perfect. I will own fiberglass boats.

Now, I'm sure many traditionalists are harumphing my like of fiberglass. After all, just as there are those with devotions to traditional bows or split bamboo fly rods, there are those equally loyal to wooden boats. Now it would seem that with my own liking for wooden bars and wooden buildings and wooden piers that wooden boats would also capture my passion, and if truth be known, I find wooden boats to be the most beautiful crafts on the water. I have taken to reading

Wooden Boat magazine and staring longingly at the photos contained therein. *Wooden Boat* is my fantasy magazine. I find myself dreaming about wooden boats. I've long wanted to head up to Wooden Boat School in Brookline, Maine, or to The Aques School in Sausalito, California, or North West School of Wooden Boat Building in Port Townsend, Washington, or The Landing School of Boatbuilding and Design just outside of Kennebunkport, Maine, to learn the skills required to produce these magnificent crafts. Whether it's a 43′ Cutter, 68′ Trumpy, Old Town dink, Devlin Oarling dory, 43′ Penbo trawler, 30′ Bayhead skiff, Chris-Craft Constellation, McKenzie drift boat, or 15′ kayak, I lust after wooden boats. I long for the feel of a teak deck warmed by a Caribbean sun. However, I spent one summer assisting a repairman who worked exclusively on wooden boats, and I learned that if you own one, all of your time must be dedicated to that boat. With fiberglass, you get to go fishing once in a while. And patching gelcoat and fiberglass is a world easier than patching dry-rot wood. And to be honest about it, I find absolutely nothing in the world more tedious than keeping teak oiled.

But let me also note that while I fantasize a good deal about the boats that appear on the pages of *Wooden Boat*, depicted as the classics, the purity of boating, I am conscious of the fact that *Wooden Boat* seeks to capitalize on a particular market. The truth is, the branches of the outdoor industry which seek to maintain tradition, to preserve what was once honorable about boating, about outdoorsmanship, also contribute to the larger problem of the industrialization of the outdoors and outdoor activities. This, of course, is not an innovative observation. Aldo Leopold wrote gracefully about the impending industrialization of outdoorsmanship more than fifty years ago. Like Leopold, I am beginning to question the effect of the growing industry not on the tools of outdoorsmanship—which seem to become more efficient and more high-tech with each catalog I receive. I am concerned as to what the word "outdoorsmanship" has come to mean.

Until recently, when one ventured into the wild, be it for sport, recreation, or survival, one did so with only minimal accessories. One only carried the necessities. One relied on one's skill and ability. A hunter, as Leopold points out in *A Sand County Almanac*, would carry only one gun, take careful shots so as not to waste ammunition. Before the advent of gunpowder, hunters made their weapons—a skill on which most hunters could not now rely should their firearm malfunction and it become necessary that they kill their game. Anglers would carry a single outfit, just enough tackle to get through the day. Yet today, we load packs and tackle boxes and dry storage compartments and truck beds with gadgets and extras and those just-in-case items. I wonder about the outdoorsman who carries so much civilization into the wild that he loses touch with why he would venture there in the first place. I am mortified by the television commercials which depict a campsite powered by a generator, complete with refrigerator, electric lights, and a television so one doesn't have to miss the big game.

Leopold too wondered about such things. He writes, "Civilization has so cluttered [the] elemental man-earth relation with gadgets and middlemen that awareness of it is growing dim. We fancy that industry supports us, forgetting what supports industry." I agree. We forget that the industry which has evolved around outdoor activities often loses sight that the primary goal of escaping into the wild is the wild, not the snowmobile or rifle scope or GPS or waterproof tent. Without the wild world, the outdoor industry would collapse, would serve no community. And so when I boast of my grandfather's contribution to this industry, I want to also point out that above all else, my grandfather has been adamant that first and foremost we must protect our waters. Without good water, boats are of no use.

We must become critical of our engagement with the outdoor industry; we must first and foremost be outdoors enthusiasts, with our emphasis on the outdoors. Leopold again: "There is value in any experience that exercises those ethical restrains collectively called 'sportsmanship.' Our tools for the pursuit of wildlife improve faster than we do, and sportsmanship is a voluntary limitation in the use of these armaments. It is aimed to augment the role of skill and shrink the role of gadgets in the pursuit of wild things." He goes on:

> *I do not pretend to know what is moderation, or where the line is between legitimate and illegitimate gadgets. It seems clear, though, that the origin of gadgets has much to do with their cultural effects. Homemade aids to sport or outdoor life often enhance, rather than destroy, the man-earth drama; he who kills a trout with his own fly has scored two coups, not one. I use many factory-made gadgets myself. Yet there must be some limit beyond which money-bought aids to sport destroy the cultural value of sport.*

The value of sport. I am intrigued at the notion of value which Leopold ascribes to sport, to nature. It seems almost counter to the very concepts to which I infer a majority of the outdoor industry ascribes.

I have spent a good deal of time at boat shows, outdoor shows, and fishing shows sponsored by magazines, environmental groups, boat companies, and many other organizations. I am always intrigued by the amount of money that is exchanged at such shows; I am amazed by the gadgets which people sell and even more so by the ones people buy. I wander around shows watching individuals convince others that their fishing will improve tenfold if they only owned an underwater fish-spotting camera (a mere $1500) or a new high-gloss-poly-something-or-another topwater jig. Everyone is trying to cash in. Roy and I attended the Dallas boat show recently, and as we walked around drooling over the big offshore fishing boats and cringing at the price tags attached to them, Roy reminded me of something very important. He told me that owning one of those big boats would sure be nice, but you could catch just as many fish in a small cheap boat. He's right. Wandering around those shows, so many lose sight of the fact that despite all of the gelcoat and stainless steel and graphite and electronics and acrylic lures, fishing still comes down to one person and one fish. I would gladly forfeit the use of all of the gadgets to ensure that I still had those moments of fish and water and struggle. I would give up fiberglass to keep the experience of wind and wave.

I have turned to Leopold's words here because they offer the very sort of inspiration which helps me not to lose sight of the important stuff, not to get lost in the industry, in the gadgets. Leopold reminds me of why I fish, of why I go rambling, of why I love being out there. But he also reminds me of why I can be proud of my grandfather in the same moment. I conclude here with his words, since they are so important and so telling: "I have the impression that the American sportsman is puzzled; he doesn't understand what is happening to him. Bigger and better gadgets are good for industry, so why not for outdoor recreation? It has not dawned on him that outdoor recreations are essentially primitive, atavistic; that their value is a contrast-value; that excessive mechanization destroys contrasts by moving the factory to the woods or to the marsh."

Education

Only once has my father asked me to commit what could be construed as an act of violence and destruction. We had watched three men stretch about a hundred yards of gill-net from the beach into the surf of the Outer Banks of North Carolina. The day before, my brothers and father and I had run along the beach a few miles further south tossing suffocating rays and other "by-kill" back into the Atlantic as a different group of netters pulled the dying animals from their nets and tossed them to the sand to die in the sun. As we watched these three men set their net, Dad and I cursed quietly. Only hours before had we tried to figure out why the fish—which were usually abundant in front of our cottage—had literally disappeared overnight. Now we knew. In the summers, we caught migrating speckled trout, bluefish, stripers, Spanish mackerel, redfish, and other species as they moved south through the surf. The nets had effectively cut off the migration.

As we sat on the cottage deck and watched the dusky shadows take over the beach, Dad's anger at the netters grew. He asked me to wait until dark, to wait until the men had sufficiently worn themselves out on the cans of Coors which were being crumpled and tossed into the surf, and to slide into the water with my snorkel gear and my knife and destroy that net.

My father is not a violent man. Before retiring, he was a criminologist at Old Dominion University, and encouraging others to break laws and act violently generally goes against his nature. Let me be clear, though: my father certainly taught us to avoid fighting when we could, but that some people just needed a good womping. Had it not been for the Mossberg with which the three men guarded their net, which dissuaded us from going through with the plan, I believe my father would have regarded the vandalistic destruction of another's property with approval that night. That was part of what he taught me: that certain fights are worth fighting. Others are not. And once in a while we have to stick our necks out to stand up for what is right. This lesson, the education of that night on the beach, has been important to me.

I once wrote a short story based on that night, based on what would have happened had I slid into the surf and taken my knife to the nets. But in the real-life version we sat and watched the men as they built a campfire and watched over their net. We went to bed that night knowing that there would be no reason to rise early, to don our waders, to cast bucktails into the surf with the hope that a fish might grace us with a strike. There would be no fish. The following morning, when we did wander out on to the cottage deck, the men, their net, and the shotgun were gone. In their place, a pile of dead rays, stripers, and other assorted animals now lay rotting. As I have learned, the logic that many netters employ is to kill anything that they can't sell, or can't legally keep, so that the next time they set the net those same fish won't waste their time by becoming snagged. So, overfished populations like striped bass, which are illegal to keep, are tossed to the sand to die. Small rays and skates that have no commercial value, too, are left to die.

I am baffled by the logic that suggests that killing all of the by-catch will prevent catching it someday in the future, that it is more productive to inflict genocide on particular species simply because they can't be sold. The concept of destroying particular parts of ecosystems in order that they not interfere with profit is ignorant, to say the least. There is no regard for the system of life in which these animals must participate and affect, and even less for the animals themselves. Certainly sharks and rays and turtles are going to damage nets; they are, after all fighting for their lives. I don't blame them one bit. But to the commercial fisherman who looks at the damaged net as an economic setback and decides that the thrashing animal is simply a direct threat to his livelihood, the desire to slaughter that which harms his nets becomes a powerful force. And for those of us who care about such things, who want to slide into the water and slash those nets, we must operate from an informed position. We must educate ourselves about the important things. We must know what is at stake with each battle before we choose if and how to fight them.

Just after Karl Wickstrom and his supporters (myself included) voted to ban in-shore commercial gill netting in Florida (the Save Our Sealife amendment passed in 1992), I heard a story about a commercial fisherman who had begun to argue that the net ban was going to backfire and would eventually kill off more species of fish than commercial fishing. His claim, it seemed, was that the indiscriminate killing inflicted by gill nets was also responsible for slaughtering a large number of gaff-tail sailcats. These catfish, he claimed, eat large quantities of trout eggs, and since there would be no population control over the cats, they would eat a larger number of trout eggs and thereby reduce the trout population. Logic, it seems, is not big with commercial netters.

Of course, we have seen countless wildlife management efforts in which the removal of certain numbers of a species helps reduce pressure put on ecosystems by overgrown populations. However, to argue that the intentional protection of a species would in turn destroy other protected species in the same system defies logic. There is no thought of consequence and action. No thought of nature.

I've recounted earlier the numbers of times I've witnessed this same logic in smaller proportions on piers up and down the East Coast. The "kill 'em so we don't catch em again" mentality is alive and well among sport anglers as well. The numbers of times I've witnessed sailcats, rays, sharks, skates, sea robins, rockfish, and countless other "nuisance" fish killed so anglers might avoid catching them again is astronomical. Granted, the numbers do not even come close to the numbers of by-catch killed by commercial netters and long liners. Yet, it is even in these instances of singular fish being killed that we must begin to direct our efforts. Let me explain:

Early October. Friday, just after midnight. The moon is full as Roy and I barrel across State Road 60 from Tampa to Winter Haven. A sack of jerky sits between us on the truck bench, and we pull pieces from the bag and tear at the dry meat with our incisors. Chewing the salty flesh and washing it down with Coke (to which both of us are addicted), we ramble about everything and nothing: school, politics, fishing, women, music. We are headed for Sebastian and the rumor of big reds.

In Winter Haven, we jump on 92 and curse the neon and the fact that there's so much traffic in Kissimmee even at one in the morning. The conversation turns to the unnecessary growth not just in Kissimmee but all over the state. We take turns yelling at Canadian drivers from behind closed windows so they don't really hear us. Snow bird season is just in its opening days. No bag limits. From 92 it's on to 192 and into Melbourne. Our plan is to hit Sebastian just after three in the morning with two bait buckets filled with pinfish purchased at Whitey's on our way down A1A and to fish without a break until Sunday afternoon. If we need sleep, we'll sleep on the pier; lord knows it won't be the first time or the most uncomfortable pier on which we've slept.

When we get to Whitey's, they're closed for the few hours they actually lock the doors, and we wait for an hour in the parking lot, still tearing and gnawing on jerky. When the doors open at Whitey's we're there ready for bait; our five-gallon buckets opened and waiting to receive dip-nets full of pinfish. We hit the pier, gear in tow, a good hour before the sun starts to give hints of its arrival. The few others who have stayed the night, or arrived earlier than we, are chatting lively about how great yesterday was, but were bemoaning the fact that things slowed at about midnight. We baited hooks, set baits in the water, started working gold spoons, and waited.

As the sun began to rise over the slow rolling swells of an autumn Atlantic, the weekend crowds began to arrive. By ten, the pier was stacked shoulder to shoulder, and bottom fishermen were hauling in trout, black drum, small blues, small Spanish, and a host of other species. But there had been no reds.

By eleven, the reds returned in small numbers. Now those targeting reds were getting excited, but the crowded pier, the force of Sebastian's strong tides, and the variety of rigs being used caused one tangle after another. Roy and I were forced to fish a good distance apart in order to find enough space to cast. I could tell Roy was getting angry. Too many people, too many tourists, too many fish being killed. Every animal that was hooked, whether legal or not, found its way into someone's bucket. I pulled in an undersized trout and immediately some guy with a heavy Yankee accent asked if I planned on keeping it. Upon my reply that I intended to release the fish, he asked if he could have it. I just shook my head and put the fish back in the water.

By noon, I had hooked and lost one decent sized red. Roy was not pleased with me for losing it. I had switched to my 15-foot surf casting outfit, hoping to be able to cast beyond the tangle of other anglers' lines. But when the red finally came close enough to net, the added length of the rod gave just enough spring to allow the fish to throw the hook. Roy insisted that I return to a smaller rod.

Five minutes later, Roy brought a beautiful 30-inch red to deck. While I was snapping photos of Roy and the first of three reds he'd take that day, the same Yankee tourist asked Roy if he could have the fish. Roy, in one of the most profound moments I've ever witnessed, looked the guy in the eye, said with a calm conviction that made me proud, "No, you people have killed enough today," tossed the fish back in, and walked away with his head down.

When I saw Roy drop his head, I knew something was wrong. I looked, too, to the pier deck where his eyes now focused. It was scattered with dead mullet, rays, skates, shrimp, pinfish, greenbacks, grunts, drum, Spanish, blues, flounder, and just about every other species found in the waters around Sebastian.

Roy was right. There had been enough killed that day. There had been enough killed, I'm sure, that week, and that weekend filled with tourists and weekend anglers would prove to kill even more. There is little ethical consideration on a crowded Saturday pier. The problem, however, extends beyond a simple ethical position we must take when fishing. It extends to a point of education, to an understanding of not just why we must be careful in our harvesting, but an understanding of where that harvesting fits on larger scales. That is, when we fish, we must educate ourselves beyond the beauty of the fish, beyond the complexities and simplicities of the activity of fishing, beyond the know-how of tackle, beyond the knowledge of species. We must look at the bigger picture, the role of humans in the world of fish, and in turn, in the world of all that lives.

What Roy reminded me that day was that despite our love for fishing, at some point, our fun—not just mine and Roy's, but all of ours—must be considered in relation to the survival of natural environments. It is very easy for us to pick targets that we can identify as environmentally destructive—Jet Skis, long liners, gill netters, loggers, and such—but it is of equal if not greater importance that we take the time to learn about why these targets cause damage and what we as a community can do to prevent such destruction. Part of this education comes from a critical eye to what we are told.

When *Florida Sportsman* editor Karl Wickstrom initiated the Save Our Sealife campaign in April of 1991, his intentions were clear from the beginning: to introduce legislation that would regulate the use of nets by commercial fishermen in Florida's costal waters. This initiative drew distinct battle lines: on the one side stood the sportfishing industry as defenders of the environment—the good guys. On the other side stood the environmental pillaging commercial fishermen—the bad guys. With Wickstrom and *Florida Sportsman* promoting other pieces of legislation following SOS, it is crucial that we outdoor enthusiasts examine the issues so that we might provide strong support, not just for Wickstrom, should we align ourselves with his agendas, but for any conservation effort we deem necessary. While Wickstrom and his supporters were able to impose legislation in July of 1995 that will undoubtedly have extremely beneficial environmental impact, we have to look to the future and other environmental debates. I hope that conservationists, environmentalists, and outdoor enthusiasts will continue to support efforts like Wickstrom's both in Florida and in the rest of the world, and

I hope that we will all do so with a conscious awareness of the very words that suggest *why* we act as we do.

The argument for banning inshore commercial netting was simple: certain types of commercial nets inflicted considerable damage to fish populations due to extreme harvesting practices. In addition, these nets were responsible for unnecessary killing of marine mammals like porpoises and manatees. SOS argued that curtailing the use of inshore gill nets would help Florida's economy since both commercial and recreational fishing relied on healthy fish populations, particularly mullet populations.

Opponents to the ban argued that there had been no collapse in mullet fisheries. Sport fishermen knew otherwise. There has been a visible decrease not only in numbers of harvested mullet, but in numbers of fish populations which rely on mullet for food. Coupled with this decrease in fish populations were the actions I witnessed as I worked outdoor and boat shows (at the time, I was a field editor with Florida's *The Fisherman* magazine), during which small groups of enraged net fishermen would assault and harass ban-the-net supporters and leave them bloodied on the floor as they shouted "Don't kill our families!" And, as a sportsman, I saw the intentional destruction of fish populations in threatening retaliation against supporters of the ban. I saw what such an enviro-political battle can do to people, to Florida.

The SOS debate, when whittled away, is merely a problem generated by the way people think and act in cultural units: what our culture defines as the appropriate way to make use of fish stock. But, within ecologically conscious conventional wisdom, we equate environmental issues with moral standards, with the choices our culture and other cultures make. Briefly put, the dilemma is this: what is the morally correct position? To preserve fish populations or to make use of them? The difficulties of the SOS dilemma are compounded further because the ethical problem issues from a more crucial problem: that of humankind's place in the natural world. In an oversimplified version: on one side a group (the net fishermen) is depicted as viewing nature as a warehouse of resource for human use, while the opposing culture sees people as having an intrusive, yet sustainable, role in the earth's ecosystems.

As much as the ban-the-nets debate is a problem of ethics, cultural heritage, and economic survival, it is also a problem of words. Different proposals to resolve the crisis are forwarded by the competing social groups or cultures—all with varying sources of information, needs, beliefs, divergent goals, methods, and values. Each culture has a particular perspective and uses a specialized language developed specifically to express their view of the world and, in this case, to convince others that their's is the more moral, the more correct.

Thankfully, making a choice in this debate was simple: banning inshore gill-netting was the right thing to do. Florida's voters, thanks to the information provided by Wickstrom and others, took the time to understand why such an action needed to take place.

Voting to ban the nets was, in fact, a very courageous move on behalf of Florida voters. Rarely, do we as a state move away from a money-making industry. Florida, traditionally, has been a state where high-dollar ethics prevail. I note the tourist industry and the sugar industry as prime examples. However, in the case of SOS, the voters of Florida were willing to acknowledge that while a certain population would suffer economically, it was time that we stop harming our own resources. Such an endeavor was needed, and it was encouraging to see Florida voters take what they had learned and finally take a stand.

We must look to the information that is provided us. We must think about the rhetoric, about the language. We must be willing, no matter who we stand facing, to say "there's been enough killing here." We must be willing to acknowledge that certain fights are worth fighting, and we must have the courage to fight them. And we must not forget, as Marjorie Kinnan Rawlings wrote, that "We were bred of earth before we were born of our mothers. Once born, we can live without mother or father, or any other kin, or any friend, or any human love. We cannot live without the earth or apart from it, and something is shriveled in a man's heart when he turns away from it and concerns himself only with the affairs of men."

Sea Sick

There are certain things anglers never want to have to admit. Getting skunked pretty much tops the list. When asked the questions asked of all anglers—"Did you get anything?" "Any luck?" "How'd you do?" "They biting?"—rarely will you hear, "We got skunked." Getting the skunk out of the boat, as they say, is an important thing to do early on.

Fisherfolk are notorious for creatively withholding the "I got skunked" response. I have a Ph.D. in rhetoric, but even a trained professional like me can learn from anglers of the world about how not to say something straight out. The responses are well-known and well-rehearsed, to be uttered with the greatest conviction of the speaker so as not to raise suspicion and to turn the conversation elsewhere: "Nothing worth mentioning." "Nothing we could keep." "Did alright, but not as good as yesterday." "Missed the tide." "Some small stuff." "A few." We've all heard these lines before; we've all used them before. A true angler knows how to interpret these responses and would never push a brother or sister fisher to elaborate, clarify, or qualify. A novice or a nosey tourist, however, may continue to interrogate and inevitably force an angler into an uncomfortable position wherein he or she may teeter near the truth and risk reputation as angler and liar. A real pro can always avoid the subject with the classic: "I'm getting a beer; you need one?"

The other thing fisherfolk are slow to admit to is getting seasick. Perhaps part of the reason is that if you get seasick in front of someone else—a fishing buddy, a family member, a complete stranger—that person will undoubtedly report your misery to anyone—other fishing buddies, family members, or complete strangers ("Hey you!, You shoulda seen my brother hurling out there")—as soon as possible, at length, and with great detail. Usually entirely too much detail. For some reason the degree of one's suffering from seasickness is proportional to the glee and humor others find in hearing about or witnessing your pain. "Feeding the fish" or "chumming" as we anglers euphemistically refer to this agony, is uncharacteristically funny to nonsufferers.

Maybe this isn't the thing to do in the world of fisherfolk, in a world where I'd like to be able to write and wander safely, but I want to admit that I get seasick. I don't mean that occasionally I get a little nauseous; I mean that from time to time, when I get on big water, I get fucking seasick. The fish are well fed; my head aches; my stomach attempts to exit my body through any orifice it can reach, including my ears; my eyes decide to give me quick glimpses of what shishkababed tomatoes feel like; and each muscle in my body figures now would be a good time to pay me back for any abuse I might have inflicted upon it in the past thirty years. I experience complete body mutiny. "Attention body parts. We're headed for the open sea; all parts womp him where you can!" All the while, I am convinced that dying is a really reasonable solution, that death is the best option. I have even asked my brother to just pitch me overboard in a squall and let me drown. Not knowing much about death, as I mentioned earlier in this book, I am certain that I'd rather be dead than be seasick.

For just about any fisherman, such a display of water intolerance would be embarrassing. Lord knows I've laughed shamelessly at others as they begged me to shoot them. In fact, I must confess, I've even ridiculed my own mother, who is notorious for getting seasick, as she was offering up a tropical buffet for our piscatorial friends. Among the lore of clan Dobrin is a tale my grandfather tells often at family gatherings of a fishing trip he made with my father and mother years before my birth. As the story goes, my grandfather had purchased a large load of sardines from a commercial boat and had begun chumming the water off of Jacksonville Beach when kingfish started blasting out of the water by the dozens. The more sardines he threw, the more kingfish slashed the chum slick. As tens of thousands of smoker kings (remember this is my grandfather's story and according to him there must have been millions of kings around) began circling his boat, he and Dad excitedly grabbed rods and were just getting ready to cast into the now solid mass of kingfish.

At that moment, from the stern came a mighty bellow, a sound that would later be reported to have been mistaken for a foghorn and caused the wrecks of seven trollers and two ocean liners. As near as my grandfather can imitate, the sound was a deep, resounding "RRRAAAAOOOOUUUUULLLL-LLFFFFFFF," much like a thousand-pound lion dying a miserable death in echoed bass with the reverb turned all the way up. Since my father had not yet been witness to my mother's morning sickness, and since neither he nor my grandfather had ever heard such a horrible sound uttered by anything in the natural world, they wheeled around expecting to see some ancient sea monster about to devour their boat. Instead, they were witness to one of the most elaborate displays of seasickness on record. To this day, small triggerfish, clownfish, parrotfish, and other reef feeders still find small morsels from the day known to all fish as the day of the great feeding. Old grandparent fish still tell young schools the legend of the day they all ate like kings (sorry, bad pun). Manna from mama. My mother, without speaking, was able to order my father and grandfather to return to the dock; she has an uncanny ability to look an order at you. My grandfather still grieves over the day he could have caught a million kingfish, but each time the story is told, just as he is ready to blame and curse my mother for that loss, a sudden shiver of a memory rocks his frame and he refuses to speak any more of that day.

For a writer, such events make great stories, though I don't recall any of the great writers ever waxing poetic about seasickness. However, for a writer who writes about fishing to also be a sufferer of seasickness, well, let's just say that's not a career boost. When I first started writing for *The Fisherman*, my editor Andy Dear asked if I would represent the magazine at an editor/writers gathering sponsored by Bear Advertising, who handled Suzuki motors and Penn rods and reels. Of course, I said yes. At the time I had no idea what to expect; I had never written professionally for a magazine.

Several major saltwater fishing magazines were represented, and Bear did a wonderful job providing boats, tackle, guides, food, and lodging. Every other writer showed up prepared to take roll after roll of film of fish displayed in front of Suzuki engines and next to Penn tackle. When I arrived the first morning carrying my $35 instamatic camera, I got a few looks that noted I either didn't belong there or was one hell of an amateur. To make matters worse, on the first day I was among the group to go offshore in search of grouper. The guide was renowned for knowing spots in the Gulf of Mexico that held grouper the size of apartment buildings.

I was thankful we were on the west coast of Florida since I had never been seasick on the Gulf before. The Gulf is, after all, notoriously flat. But just as we left view of land, my body once again sent out the call "Open water ho! Commence to womping!" And the inner rumblings of the mutiny began. With only two small grouper on board for later photo shoots, the kind guide noticed that I had stopped fishing and was turning various shades of colors resembling the paint used on the insides of prisons and that some of my breakfast was forcing its way between my fingers, which were clasped tightly over my mouth. Without alerting anyone to my condition he announced that today wasn't the day for grouper fishing and that we should go back inside to look for snook. Unfortunately, we were in a deep-v hull and the guide knew absolutely nothing about fishing the mangrove areas around Boca Grande, though he did find us a few snapper around the railroad trellis and phosphate pier.

Thinking I had escaped a career-ending embarrassment, George Poveromo of *Saltwater Sportsman* fame, the Bear Advertising executives, the owner of Mirr-O-Lure, a few other writers, and I had a pleasant dinner that night back at the dock after I snapped a few pictures of the two armadillo-sized grouper admiring a Suzuki outboard. The next night, however, in front of the same crowd, the nice people at Bear presented me with some due ribbing and a certificate which read, "Most improved angler. After all, with a start like that, it couldn't get any worse."

The certificate still hangs in my study; and I never did get to write a story about that trip for *The Fisherman*. I will say that the next few days were filled with some of the best snook fishing I have ever experienced. And in order to fulfill the promise I made about plugging Penn and Suzuki in my writing, I still fish with Penn rods and reels. However, I don't own a Suzuki outboard, though I would gladly use one should the nice fellows down at Bear Advertising want to send me one (something in a short-shaft 90 horsepower would do nicely).

I won't continue telling seasick stories, though doing so might be fun, and the challenge of regurgitating the events with the appropriately colorful descriptions might appeal to my writerly sense. I am thankful that modern medicine has spent a good deal of energy on searching for cures to motion sickness. I still don't understand how all of those explorers like Bering or Vespucci got on those tiny little ships and sailed out into big water without the aid of pharmaceuticals. At the time of the great Bear Advertising upchuck, I was aware of no other response to my affliction than suffering or Dramamine. Unfortunately, I can eat the tiny little pills like M&Ms with no effect other than spoiling my appetite, so suffering was about my only option. Once, while sailfishing in a wintery Atlantic, I tried using the Transderm Scop patches that you put behind your ear and they release a chemical into your skin. They seemed to work, but my doctor swore they had bad side effects and wouldn't write me any more prescriptions. I never suffered any side effect other than not puking while at sea and was sorry to have to find a new doctor.

A few years ago my father got a prescription for a drug called Meclizine (pronounced No-vomit-all) which was reported to "shut off the vomit centers in your brain." The way it was explained was that Meclizine didn't keep you from feeling seasick, it just kept you from vomiting; your body literally would lose its ability to purge. My brother and I decided to try the new pills while fishing aboard a head boat out of Port Canaveral one winter. Sure enough, most everyone on board got seasick, including a couple of Japanese fellows who showed up to fish wearing expensive slacks, Italian leather loafers, and leather sports coats. They puked all over themselves and never lifted a rod. For the record, Italian leather does not stave off vomit too well, and the softer chunks seem to mush into the leather work.

Adam and I, however, never puked. There were moments when I really, really wanted to, but I couldn't. My body had forgotten how. The damn pills worked. I was still sick; I still wanted to die. I wanted some release, but the catharsis of vomit could not happen because of the damn pills. The mutineers were rendered weaponless. Of course, no one else on the boat knew I was sick since I wasn't puking, so I was saved from embarrassing myself in front of the Japanese tourists. Adam and I sat next to them and pretended to drink beer, and we slung squid and dead bait around to add to the head boat aroma just to rub it in a little.

This past winter, while diving in the Keys with my family, I decided to take a radical approach to seasickness prevention. I took a mixture of Triptone, Dramamine, and Meclizine in double doses of each. Despite my mother's certainty that I would be dead from an overdose, I never got seasick, and we faced seven to nine foot seas. For three days I took my drug cocktail, and for three days I never felt a twinge of seasickness. My mother, however, puked so badly on the first day she refused to set foot on the boat the rest of the trip, though her display on the first day was epic and brought fish from around Florida who had heard the stories from their grandparents of the day in Jacksonville.

I suppose making fun of my mother in print is not the kindest thing I could do. After all, I must confess, Mom put a great deal of effort into teaching me and my brothers about the sea. I distinctly remember her standing me in front of a churning Atlantic when I was little and telling me, "There's the ocean. Respect her and she will treat you well. Disrespect her and she will kill you." I have never forgotten that. In fact, I think that's an important lesson that we all should learn and should teach our children. If you don't respect the ocean, she will kill you. I'm not sure about the gendering of the water, but I like it so I'm going to stick with it. After all, there is something incredibly maternal about large bodies of salt water. Whenever something is bothering me, or I have to make an important decision, I have to have salt water. In many ways, for me, it's like going to Mom when something's bothering me. Out here in Kansas, the only salt water I have is a two-liter bottle of Gulf water that I brought with me. It's not the same as the Gulf or the ocean, but in a pinch I can sprinkle a taste of it on my face and work my way through the tougher decisions.

But, as I said, we all need to take my mother's words to heart. All of us, not just those who were fortunate enough to grow up within the reaches of salt spray, but all of us. For those of us who did grow up on the world's beaches, we know what rough water, undertows, flood tides, and other little ocean nasties can do. We have all risked drowning; many of us have seen it happen. And surely we have seen the havoc rough water can wreak upon boats and beach houses. But this isn't really the message I take from my mother's words these days. Sure, big water can be a dangerous place for the novice or for damned fools who run boats too fast, or drink while on the water, or who swim without waiting 30 minutes after eating, but these words mean so much more today.

Our oceans—by *ours*, I mean the world's—are sick. We have lost the respect we need for our oceans. Humans have taken to dumping all sorts of things in salt waters that don't belong there. We flush millions of gallons of pollutants; we dump barges of trash; we let septic tanks leak. All into our oceans. Now I don't know about you, but if anyone was dumping their waste into my house, I would consider it a disrespectful action. I would also mop up the mess with that person's head, inverting them so as to serve as a human mop—a cleaning process I witnessed a former Green Beret sniper use when he caught a guy with dreadlocks eating his dinner. That sort of lack of respect begs punishment. So too does the disrespect humans have shown for the world's oceans. The problem here is that continued disrespect for these waters will literally kill us. Our oceans are critical to world ecosystems, and our seas are sick.

I may joke in these pages about what humans regurgitate into our waters, but the truth is we are throwing a lot more into them than a few chunks of partially digested bologna sandwiches. Our oceans now contain contaminants such as DDT, the horrible pesticide which Rachel Carson warned us about in her classic 1962 book *Silent Spring*. Traces of PCBs and nuclear waste, too, can be found in our waters. Countless oil spills, which don't gain the attention of big spills such as the now famed *Exxon Valdez* disaster, leave an ever-growing quantity of petroleum in our oceans. And this is just the big stuff.

I find this frightening. These waters are our life source. Salt water courses through our blood—literally. If we kill the oceans, we kill ourselves. The oceans themselves are blood, just as the wind is breath. The idea is not new; primitive through modern cultures have made similar claims. James Lovelock, in his two books *Gaia* and *Ages of Gaia*, does a wonderful job of constructing the world-as-living-organism argument. We need to listen, to know that we need our oceans.

What's frightening is that it's not just large companies and industrial by-product. Individuals regularly toss unimaginable quantities of crap into our oceans. Every time I fish or dive or just walk down a beach, I find myself gathering up loads of garbage left by individuals who simply have no respect. I liken this to disrespecting one's mother and think the penalty for littering on, in, or, near our oceans should rival the Spanish Inquisition's punishment for heresy. I am tired of picking up plastic wrappers, plastic cups, aluminum cans, golf balls, fishing line, towels, aluminum foil, and the tons of other shit people throw into the ocean. Rarely when I dive in salt water do I return from the bottom without my BCD pockets filled with the same trash one finds in dumpsters at housing complexes. This stuff does not belong on our reefs; it does not belong on our beaches. I do not dive to pick up trash; I dive to see reefs, not reefs bespeckled with sandwich bags and soda cans. My message to those of you throwing your trash on the beach or overboard is simple: knock it off.

This is a message I've recently decided to no longer keep to myself. This past winter, I was visiting my parents and brothers in Cocoa Beach for the semester break. (No one, especially a blue water bum such as myself, should have to suffer an entire Kansas winter. Those of you who live even farther north in uninhabitable places like Minnesota or Ohio or some God-forsaken place like Canada, let me remind you that the human animal evolved from having hair on its body for a reason. We were not meant to live in that kind of cold; we are tropical animals.) While out driving one day, I watched a couple toss hamburger wrappers and soda cans from their car window on to the causeway at Merrit Island. Furious to see such a disregard for an area that is partly my home and a part of all of the salt waters I think of as home, I pulled the truck up next to the shitheads and began hollering at them to pick up their crap. Now, I'd like to be able to report that the individuals in the car were of the French-Canadian persuasion, since I'd like nothing more than to gripe about the snowbird presence in Florida, but these particular idiots were driving a car with Polk County Florida tags. Locals. Somewhat. When I began to point out their disregard for our state, they shrugged, rolled up the windows, and simply ignored me. This is perhaps the most infuriating tactic one can take with someone who is angry with you; it is a tactic I have used a countless number of times. Needless to say, my anger and exasperation became overwhelming. I was deciding on the best way to smash the driver-side window with what was handy, when the two drove away, smiling and waving a final   we-really-don't-give-a-fuck-about-what-you-think goodbye. Oh for my 12 gauge at that moment. Justifiable buckshotting of a Japanese two-door.

Unfortunately, this is an all too familiar scene in America these days, not just on beaches or near water. Not two days ago, the truck and I were tooling along looking for a couple of bald eagles that nest out here on this thing they call "Lake Clinton." Leaving Truckzilla, as it has been dubbed, I slogged around in the mud looking for the birds. I noticed a couple of students having a roadside picnic on the hood of their car parked nearby, just off of the main road. As they were preparing to leave, the female of the couple gestured to the male, and as I couldn't hear her from where I stood, I assumed she had asked what to do with the trash from the meal. He, in his masculine determination, took the trash from her and tossed to the ground. Just as they rolled down their windows and began to back out onto the street, I scooped up the bundle of wrappers and cans and tossed them into the car to the driver's lap. "This is not your garbage can," I proclaimed. Startled, he began to yell and put on a show of prowess in front of his girlfriend, who was shrieking for him to drive away. I assume the show was more for her benefit than mine, as I tapped my binoculars and waited to see what would happen next. Apparently, large men with muddy boots and field jackets who step from the bushes holding binoculars are seen as a deadly threat in Kansas, because both driver and passenger were obviously scared, though he was making a feeble attempt at not letting it show. The guy decided his girlfriend was probably right and finished backing onto the road, all the while cursing and threatening to kick my ass, though he was rolling the window up as fast as he could. Just as the car hit the road and slipped into gear, all of the garbage came flying out the passenger-side window along with a definitive, "Fuck you, freak!"

"Fuck me," I thought. Hmm. "Freak." Maybe so. But, I walked down the road, picked up their crap, and tossed it into the garbage can standing not ten feet from where they had been parked. Half of me hopes to see that car on campus; half of me hopes not to. Most of me wishes I had the authority to run their license plate, find out who they are, call their parents, and tell them what kinds of morons they and their children must be. Parents should be responsible for their children's' stupidity; after all, kids who are parented well usually don't display such disrespect. Okay, I know there are some huge problems with saying that, but I just wanted to get a plug in for my parents and a shot off at the parents of those little punks.

When I worked at Willoughby Bay Marina in Norfolk as a teenager, the local police boat docked at the marina and I got to know the water cops fairly well. I also got to see tremendous numbers of idiots violate marine laws. Unfortunately, the cops were not always docked at the marina, as they had to patrol the waterways, so they didn't get to see all of the infractions I witnessed, though they saw plenty on their own. After I suggested that at least one of them remain at the marina and dish out tickets to meet quotas inside of an hour, the cops joked that I be deputized with the authority to spray paint "moron" down the hulls of boats whose owners violated local laws or who I just happened to deem morons. To this day, I would love to have that kind of authority. I crave the feeling of walking up to someone, flipping out a badge, and announcing, "Sorry sir, but I'm going to have to tag your vehicle with a moron sign so as to warn others of your stupidity." I would have written "Jackass" down the side of the Polk county car and "Dumbass, they put the garbage cans there for a reason" on the kids' car.

To be honest about it, I'm actually amazed at my own emotional reaction to others' littering. I consider myself a fairly laid back individual, a live-and-let-live, pour-me-another-drink kind of guy. But recently, I've found myself reacting deeply and angrily toward careless, disrespectful individuals.

Maybe I'm just getting old and curmudgeonly. But I think this kind of anger is important. I think it's critical that those of us who get angry not keep our mouths closed. I think it's critical that we get upset by the discretions of others. Without passion, nothing is accomplished. As I mentioned in the previous chapter, the only time my father ever asked me to commit an act of violence was in response to the disrespect and stupidity of another. I was glad to see my father get that angry that night. It was good to know that others close to me also get emotional about those sorts of things.

I'm not sure of the actual value of being angry all the time, but from where I'm sitting anger seems a pretty strong initiating force. Aristotle said, "those who are not angry at things they should be angry at are fools." If we didn't get angry, we wouldn't fight back. That's a damn shame too. We shouldn't have to fight. I shouldn't feel like I have to pick up others' trash. But I should get to paint "moron" on the boats of jerks.

Words 2

I come back to words. I come full circle in writing the words in this book, wanting to return to where I began. I have spent the last year wrapped up in the words of these pages, wrapped up in the words of my students here at the University of Kansas, and wrapped up in thinking about the places I miss. I have felt, in a way, helpless in regards to those places. And, try as I might, my best distance casts have not kept me tethered to home waters in satisfying ways.

Yet, completing these pages does provide some satisfaction in my reflections, in thinking about and in writing about the important things. I am reminded tonight of Hemingway's words, as I often am, when, in "The Snows of Kilimanjaro" he writes, "Now he would never write the things that he had saved to write until he knew enough to write them well. Well, he would not have to fail at trying to write them either. Maybe you could never write them, and that was why you put them off and delayed the starting."

Maybe I have not been able to write the things that I have until I was far enough away from them to see them. Perhaps I have had to be away to know these things. Distance, as it turns out, provides a remarkably clear panorama of things we don't always recognize from close proximity. "Step back from it and take a look," my college painting instructor used to say. Get some perspective.

Perspective makes it easier to put things where they belong, to see bigger pictures. In a lot of ways, fishing is about getting a better view, about taking the time to step back and put things in perspective, to figure out where we fit. I am often overwhelmed by the sensation of insignificance and miniscuality that rushes over me when I'm alone on big water, with no land in sight, and have a big fish on the line fighting for its life. It's not a frightening feeling; it is a feeling of perspective. It is remarkably comforting to be able to let go of the constraints of responsibility we place upon ourselves, to look around and see our smallness, and to be able to find comfort in the fact that it's alright to be a small part of this very big place. It gives occasion to let go of the vanity we have accumulated in thinking ourselves so big in this world and to relax in the protection of a big, familiar place. It is a sensation much like sleeping in an oversized bed or the safety of a child's hand swallowed by the hands of a father when crossing the street. I am glad for that perspective, to be reminded of where I fit.

There is a story I've heard in various incarnations about two friends taking a canoe trip down the Colorado River through the Grand Canyon; the story has become urban legend. The two paddled their way down the Colorado on a perfect day: the soft current of calm water; light, cooling breeze;

warm sun in a cloudless sky; and the beauty of being in the canyon riding the very artery which cut the magnificent, ancient ravine. Enraptured by the majesty and solitude of it all, the man paddling in the bow carefully rose to his feet, raised his arms in a triumphant V, lifted his face to the sky, and proclaimed to the miracle of the canyon, "I exist!" As the story goes, in the next instant, a bolt of lighting tore from the cloudless sky and struck the man dead. Perspective.

Words often provide that same perspective. Words give us the chance to walk around in our smallness and see how vast a world we inhabit. They let us see how others see, how others perceive, how others interpret the world. Harry Crews, who is one of the best writers in contemporary America, writes in *A Childhood: The Biography of A Place* that "nothing is allowed to die in a society of storytelling people." I like that. It reminds me of the importance of words, of telling. It is one of the reasons that I have turned to the enmeshing of writing and fishing; I have not wanted to let fishing die in my life. I have wanted to tell the stories that make me think about fishing, and I have wanted to read the stories that make me think about fishing. *Piscator non solum piscatur.* Fishing is not just about fishing; it is also about the words. It is about the telling of the tragedies and the heroic epics. It is about reading the water; it is about reading the world. Fishing is about so much more. And I am enthralled by all that is accumulated in a single instance of water and fish and hook and tension and human. Those who write fishing do so to help themselves and their readers to find perspective, to see that fishing is about so much more, to see that we are about so much more.

In a recent article in *The New York Times Book Review*, Holly Morris (whose work I want to again note as exceptional and long overdue) addresses the relationship between writing and fishing, which I also swerve in and out of in the pages of this book. Morris' words are profound. She reminds us that "Both fishing and writing are largely acts of faith; you believe that there is indeed a rich run of ideas lurking below." She goes on to say, "as writers and anglers, we labor to articulate why we do what we do, but all we really know is that if we do not engage, we are unhappy and suffer a melancholy defined only by absence."

I know this feeling, this absence. It is what has driven me to pursue memories of fish in the words of this book. I suppose that in some ways writing about fishing becomes a self-portrait, an attempt to step back and get a look at one's self. Yet writers who write of fishing are biased in painting this portrait; we want to paint ourselves as pastoral, strong, honorable, and at peace with the world. I certainly have taken comfort in writing these pages by remembering the serenity of salt water and of fish. Yet coupled with the writer's desire to paint this overly noble portrait, writing anglers (or angling writers) also want to be seen as ordinary, simplified in spirit, diverse in philosophy and in thought. I think I read that somewhere, though I can't place where. I jotted the thought down on a scrap of paper a few months ago and have been thinking a lot about balance between wanting to be primitive and noble, to be simple of life and unfathomed in thought. I'd like to believe that I came to the observation myself, but I'm sure some other author's words led me there. Lynyrd Skynyrd, after all, teaches us to "be a simple kind of man."

Nonetheless, I like the idea that when writers write they want the literature of fishing to be about balance. That is, writers want to find balance in their lives. This, then, becomes a self portrait of sorts, a means for me to find my way back to the water, a search for balance, and a means for my readers (who I hope share similar thoughts and philosophies) to dig at their own lives and to think how they would paint their watery portraits.

Just as writing reveals and makes vulnerable a place, so too does writing reveal and make vulnerable the writer. When we share our words with a public audience, we share a good portion of ourselves, we provide access to ourselves. When we write we create identity, we write ourselves into the lives of our readers. We ask our readers to wonder about us as people, to agree or disagree with our opinions, to walk alongside us for a moment, to let us share a bit of ourselves with them. And, when we write, we decide what parts of ourselves we wish to reveal; we decide how to construct that identity. We select what we are willing to make vulnerable. As anglers, some writers deliberately choose to share a uniquely solitary moment with others because those private moments give pause to our wanting to find balance. We ask readers to help us fight a fish, to become angry at the sight of a pillaged river, to care about the things about which we care, because as brothers and sisters of the angle we want to find a sense of belonging among each other. We want to find common ground on which we can communicate with others, in which we can find perspective and balance with those who share similar interests. We want to take comfort in knowing that though we may be small in the vast ocean, we are not alone.

I take to the words of fishing books and outdoor magazines to look for those very balances in others' words, and I write my own words into the story of fishing. Hemingway once wrote of his "indoor fishing season" during which he would turn to the pages of authors who wrote about fishing because he couldn't be on the water. I like the idea that reading about fishing does not constitute *not* fishing but rather simply a different type of fishing, a different season, a casting into different waters to see what is, in Morris' words, "lurking below." George Orwell, too, linked the activities of reading and fishing when his character George Bowling claimed that "Fishing certainly came first, but reading was a good second." I suppose that for writers of fishing, like Hemingway, like Orwell, like Morris, like myself (God, I've always wanted to see my name in a list like that), reading what others have to write about fishing is as important as writing our own words.

John Geirach, in *Sex, Death, and Fly-fishing* writes that "The assumption is that if you write stories about fishing, you must know more about it than the guy who reads those stories. Of course, the truth is the thing you probably know a little more about isn't fishing, but writing." I wonder what that says about those of us who do both—reading and writing, that is. I'd bet you won't find too many writers of fishing stories who weren't also readers of fishing stories.

I have taken an extended indoor fishing season here in Kansas; I have been reading and writing and thinking about the activities of writing and fishing. To be honest about it, I have enjoyed the time to reflect, to find perspective. But to be honest about it too, I would rather have the perspective that allows enough proximity for the salt spray to coat my face. One of the most important things that being away from the water has taught me is that I do not belong away from water. I should have known this was true as soon as I started booking as many trips away from Kansas as I could afford. And since I have written these pages to share my words about fishing, to expose a bit of myself (I know this is illegal in most places and that "bit" is probably more diminutive a word than a man should select in saying such things), I feel I owe my readers a final confession: a few months ago, on my thirtieth birthday, I accepted a faculty position teaching writing at the University of Florida. I am going home. I have come full circle.

Today I look back to the question that got me through these pages, my father's question about why we write about fishing, and I think about that relationship between words and water and fish. I have cast my thoughts to page after page of words and found the magic in those pages that nourishes the dreams of water and fish. I have realized that with all that is bound up in writing and in words, when we write about fishing, we are writing our signatures in the sand. Writers want their voices to be heard, their words to be read in those brief moments of human conversation.

While Walton and Hemingway and a few others may carve their signatures a bit deeper so that they remain visible longer, in the vastness of the world, even those voices are subtle and fleeting. We want to find balance and shout to the world that we are here, however briefly. And when we find the magic of fishing, many of us want our words to echo that magic. We want our words to capture and reflect the very magic which draws us to water and fish. It is the same magic which makes us recognize that when we find our balance, when we find where we fit, we must revel in that comfort and the words which meditate upon that place. It is the very sensation which makes us want to drift in the water's flow and ride the wind's current until we are home.

Epilogue
Sight Casting

Months have passed since I began preparing this manuscript to be sent to various editors and publishers, hoping it will find its way into publication. In those months, several of my good friends—who are also editors and publishers—read the original pages of this book and tendered suggestions for revisions which led to the version that you now hold. Nearly all of the early readers of this book repeated the same, flattering critique: "Why did you stop? Where is the narrator now?"

It is encouraging for an author to hear his audience ask for more, to hear them mourn the end of the words, to hear them miss the connection they have with narrator. Such comments are much more fulfilling than the "thank god, it's over" which all authors hear at some point in their careers and which all readers utter at some point during their's. I suppose that returning to an autobiographical account of one's self is the sort of reflection in which we would all like the opportunity to engage: a self-reflexivity about our own self-reflexivity. It's not often that we take the time to regard where we have been, but it is even more rare that we reflect on our reflections.

The short answer to the inquiry as to what has happened is simple: I have come home to salt water. From my front door, the Gulf of Mexico is an hour to the West; the Atlantic is an hour and a half to the East. I am a less than two hours from the river that is my home water. I have had the chance to catch reds, blues, snook, snapper, grouper, permit, trout, and more. I have dived reefs and springs. I have swum with manatees, porpoises, and sharks. I have watched (and eaten) gators. I have hiked in swamps. I have canoed and camped in La Laguna del Espirito Santo all the way back to places like Hell's Bay, Lostman's River, and Grave Yard Creek. I have ridden my long board on Christmas Day wearing nothing more than a bathing suit (and wondering if that wasn't excessive) while Kansas and the rest of the country shoveled snow. I have revisited Travis McGee and Skip Wiley. I have grown and eaten countless hot peppers. I have watched Atlantic sunrises and Gulf sunsets. I watched John Glenn leave Florida for the second time, and I wished I could go with him and look back at that perspective of our saltwater world. I have napped in the afternoon thunderstorms which roll in off of the Gulf just when siestas seem most needed. I have savored whiskey at Skippers and many other fine Florida bars. I have returned to Sugar Loaf Key and my old haunts where Hunter S. Thompson also lurks about. I have rebel yelled at Bike Week in Daytona. I have swum naked in the bioluminescence of the warm summer Gulf. I have longed for countless women on the beaches, still as inept at meeting them as I've always been. My skin has regained its dark tan; my summer feet are back. I have sand in my shoes.

Roy and Stormy have also moved back, and when their three children aren't using "Uncle Sid" as monkey bars, Roy and I are back to prowling for fish together. Stormy has convinced herself that finding me a wife is a top priority, though I think I stand a better chance at landing a grander in a bathtub than she does in her quest. In short, I have come home to salt water, and I can't stop smiling.

And now that I am back, I appreciate having been away. I am glad for the distance, for the perspective. On the day I moved into my house in Gainesville, I walked across the yard grinning and nearly giggling at the texture of the ground. It is a fine salt and pepper sand covered with a carpet of dried oak leaves that crunch when stepped on. That sound rushed me back to nursery school in Tallahassee, to the same ground of the playground, and there in my front yard, I was a child again. I was home, and everything was right and safe.

I began writing this book by saying that words are our links to the very magics which we can't even reach by distance casting. I still believe that. I have been fortunate in my relationships with words. The University of Florida, where I now teach writing, affords me the opportunity to talk with students about their own words and about the words of others. In classes about rhetoric and environment, in classes about writing and fishing, and in classes about the nature of writing, I explore with my students many facets of language and writing. And in-between classes, there is salt water. I often find myself walking across campus lost in the sunshine and cascades of Spanish moss which punctuate the campus' personality, laughing with the thought that only a year ago I was freezing my ass off in Kansas. Changes in latitudes, changes in attitudes, as Mr. Buffett professes.

It's odd now, looking back through these pages, that I haven't quoted Buffett along with the many others I do. He doesn't know it, but he's been a teacher of mine—or at least his words teach me a lot. He has taught me not just the carpe diem stuff that most people get from his sun-drenched melodies, but he's tought me about success, about achieving it, about what it really means, and mostly what a heap load of crap we associate with success. Success, in my book, is a good glass of rum punch or whiskey, a Gulf Coast sunset, and a grill full of snapper you just caught. If you have these things you had a successful day.

Buffett is a fine writer. If you want to guffaw that claim, that just tells me that you don't know his writing and you understand his work simply through the more popular songs that a few radio stations and bad bar bands play. If you want to learn Buffett, read his books; read his pieces in *Sports Afield* and in *Esquire*; pay attention to the evolution of his music beyond those few well-known songs. The man has story-teller's talents and a sound philosophy about living. Buffett is someone I want to meet, someone I want talk to, not to fawn over, not ask stupid fan questions. I imagine celebrities like him get pretty damn tired of fans sometimes. Hell, if I'm going to fawn over someone, it's going to be Jennifer Anniston or some Playboy Bunny, not another blue water bum like myself. No, with Buffett, I just want to have drinks, talk fishing and books, listen to some Robert Earl Keen or Dr. John tunes, and maybe tell a lie or two.

I've been reading Buffett's autobiographical *A Pirate Looks at Fifty* this week, and I was taken by his discussions of fly-fishing. He writes: "A fine fisherman named Lou Tabory had recently written a book on how to fly-fish the Northeast. I went out and bought it and soaked up the local knowledge about surf cast-ing and fishing the rips, but there was still one big difference— seeing what you were catching. Never fully understood by lay-men or long-liner, fly-fishing's most alluring appeal is the view." The view—this is why I have come home to salt water. If distance casting gives us the opportunity to reach as far out as we possibly can, then sight casting gives us a bit more control in our lives. Here where the water is clean and clear, where my family is near, I can target fish, cast, strip line, fight, as I see fit—literally and metaphorically. I have enjoyed the perspective that distance casting provides, and I will continue to reach for my 15-foot surf caster and send spoons and plugs as far out beyond the breakers as I can. But, these days, the thought of carefully placed casts, carefully planned words, and a little sight casting seems quite comfortable.

About the Author

A lifelong fisherman from a family of fishermen, Sid Dobrin worked for two years as a professor of English at the University of Kansas before moving on to the University of Florida, where he is currently the Director of Writing Programs. He teaches all levels of writing courses on such topics as American nature writing, environmental rhetoric, and the literature of fishing. A former field editor for Florida's *The Fisherman* magazine and contributor to *The Sportfishing Report*, he has written, co-written, edited, and co-edited more than 10 books about writing and ecology. He is currently working on a new book about fishing and post-modernity. He is also on a lifelong quest for the perfect grouper sandwich, the perfect cheeseburger, and the perfect glass of rum punch, all of which he'd enjoy on the perfect boat docked in front of the perfect beach hut.